ASTROLOGY UNVEILED

Revealing the Hidden Wisdom of Planets and the Inner Sky

SERIES VII

The stars are not distant—they are within.

SHREE SHAMBAV

ASTROLOGY UNVEILED
Revealing the Hidden Wisdom of Planets and the Inner Sky – Series VII

Shree Shambav

Published by Shree Shambav, Tamil Nadu, India

First Edition, 2025

ISBN: 978-93-343-3671-9
Email:shreeshambav@gmail.com
Web:www.shambav.org

DEDICATION

"Isavasyam idam sarvam yat kim ca jagatyam jagat, tena tyaktena bhunjitha, ma gridhah kasyasvid dhanam"

To the Almighty,

the Divine Masters,

the family who listens,

and my parents who see –

your presence shapes the pages of my life's journey.

"Isavasyam idam sarvam yat kim ca jagatyam jagat"

Meaning: "God encompasses everything you perceive, see, or touch with your sense organs."

DISCLAIMER

Astrology Unveiled – Foundations of Ancient Wisdom, Series VII is a personal exploration and reflection on the esoteric traditions of astrology. This book is the result of the author's sincere journey to interpret, understand, and convey the teachings of ancient sages and the timeless wisdom they imparted.

The content herein is intended solely for personal enrichment, introspection, and educational purposes. It reflects the author's perspectives, experiences, and interpretations, and is not presented as professional advice or a guide for astrological practice. Readers are strongly advised not to use the information in this book for professional or commercial purposes, including but not limited to counselling, diagnosis, or decision-making in personal, financial, medical, or legal matters.

The author makes no representations or warranties of any kind with respect to the accuracy, applicability, fitness, or completeness of the content. By reading this book, you acknowledge and agree that the author shall not be held liable for any loss, damage, or adverse consequences resulting from the use or misuse of the material presented.

Any discomfort, disagreement, or emotional reaction provoked by the content is entirely unintentional. Astrology is a complex and symbolic language that may intersect with deeply held beliefs; readers are encouraged to engage with the material with an open and reflective mindset.

This book is offered with the utmost respect for the reader's personal path. It is a humble invitation to contemplate ancient knowledge, not a directive to adopt or reject any belief system. Let it serve as a mirror for thought, not a mandate for action.

This book is shared in the spirit of intellectual exploration and inner reflection, and it is the reader's responsibility to discern and decide how the information resonates with their own journey.

Note: For knowledge purpose only.

Note - If any part of the book, in any sequence, hurts the reader's sentiments, it would be just out of a sheer accident not intentional

EPIGRAPH

"Above us, the stars — ancient scribes of fate.

Within us, the echo — a soul aligned with the cosmos.

To discover the power of the planets is to remember

that we, too, are celestial."

– Shree Shambav

ASTROLOGY UNVEILED

Foundations of Ancient Wisdom

SERIES VII

Discovering the Power of the Planets

SHREE SHAMBAV

Shree Shambav is a 44x best-selling author renowned for his transformative works in personal development and spiritual growth

Dear Cherished Readers

Dear Cherished Readers,

As I embark on this new literary voyage, my heart swells with profound gratitude and an overwhelming sense of connection. With deep emotion, I extend my heartfelt appreciation to each of you who has joined me on this journey.

With sincere warmth, I invite you to revisit the steps we have taken together through the pages of my earlier works. Our odyssey began with "Journey of Soul - Karma," a book that marked my first foray into the world of words and a testament to the raw passion that ignited my writing adventure.

The subsequent chapters of our shared journey unfolded through the enchanting tapestry of the *"Twenty + One"* series. With each page turned, it felt as though a brushstroke was added to the canvas of our collective imagination—stories and sentiments woven to echo within the quiet corners of your heart. These weren't just words; they were invitations to feel, to reflect, and to remember what truly matters.

And how can I not cherish the transformative path we walked together through the *"Life Changing Journey—Inspirational Quotes Series?"* Day by day, quote by quote, we ventured inward—into spaces often overlooked—to find wisdom in simplicity and light in life's shadows. Each reflection was offered as a gentle whisper of hope, a spark meant to uplift, inspire, and remind us that even in silence, the soul speaks.

The release of "Death - Light of Life and the Shadow of Death" promises to shed new light on the timeless mystery of death.

The **Optimum Python Series** is a comprehensive guide designed to empower readers at every stage of their programming journey. It begins with *Series I: Ultimate Guide for Beginners*, which lays a strong foundation in Python, making it accessible and engaging for newcomers. *Series II: Exploring Data Structures and Algorithms* takes the next step, offering a deep dive into core computer science principles that enhance problem-solving skills and coding efficiency. Building on this, *Series III: Python Power for Data Science* introduces powerful libraries such as NumPy, Pandas, Matplotlib, and Scikit-learn, guiding readers through data manipulation, visualisation, and foundational machine learning techniques. Finally, *Series IV: Unleashing the Potential of Data Science with Machine Learning Techniques* explores advanced machine learning models and real-world applications, enabling readers to harness the full potential of data-driven insights. Whether you're just starting out or looking to master sophisticated tools and strategies, this series is your roadmap to Python proficiency and beyond.

Shree Shambav expands his artistic repertoire with "*Whispers of Eternity: A Symphony of Soulful Verses*," a heartfelt exploration of the human experience. Alongside this, his "*Whispers of the Soul: A Journey Through Haiku*" distils profound insights into poignant verses. Together, these works showcase his versatility and mastery of soulful expression, inviting readers on a journey of self-discovery. Through his poetry, he weaves a rich tapestry of emotion that resonates deeply with the heart.

Shree Shambav's latest works—*Learn to Love Yourself: A Journey of Discovering Inner Beauty and Strength Through 10 Transformative Rules, The Power of Letting Go: Embrace Freedom and Happiness, A Journey of Lasting Peace—are true treasures of self-discovery, The Entitlement Trap: Get Over It, Get On, Whispers of a Dying Soul: Unspoken Regrets and Unlived Dreams, Whispers of Silence - Unlocking Inner Power through Stillness, The Power of Words: Transforming Speech, Transforming Lives, The Art of Intentional Living: Minimalism for a Life of Purpose, Awakening the Infinite:The Power of Consciousness in Transforming Life, Beyond the Veil: A Journey Through Life After Death series, Bonds Beyond Blood - Where love builds bridges, and bonds defy blood., A Journey into Spiritual Maturity - 12 Golden Rules for Inner*

Transformation, The Seeker's Gold : Unlocking Life's Greatest Treasure, , The Power of Manifestation - Unlocking The Path From Thought To Reality and Born to Rise Series.

In addition to these works, Shree Shambav has recently ventured into astrology with the release of Astrology Unveiled – Foundations of Ancient Wisdom Series I to VI, expanding into the realm of metaphysics. These books explore the foundational principles of Vedic astrology, offering readers a rich and practical understanding of this ancient wisdom.

Your unwavering support, enthusiasm to immerse yourself in my writings, and readiness to embark on these journeys with me have been my greatest sources of inspiration. Your input has been a beacon guiding me through the creation process, moulding these stories into containers of passion, emotion, knowledge, and resonance.

As I unveil this new narrative before you, know that your presence, insights, and shared moments have been my companions. The path we have walked together is etched in the annals of my creative evolution, and it's an honour beyond words to have you by my side once more.

Here's to the readers who have illuminated my path with their presence, who have embraced my stories with open hearts, and who have woven themselves into the very fabric of my literary world. Our journey has been a symbiotic dance of writer and reader, a harmony of souls brought together by the magic of storytelling.

With a heart brimming with appreciation and eyes glistening with anticipation, I extend my deepest gratitude for your unwavering support. Thank you for the memories, the shared emotions, and the countless hours spent in the worlds we've crafted together. As we step into this new adventure, let's continue to explore, feel, and discover the boundless horizons that words can unveil.

Warmly,

Shree Shambav

Suggested Reads

FROM BEST-SELLING AUTHOR

ENDORSEMENTS

"A profound and illuminating journey into the heart of ancient astrology. Astrology Unveiled is more than a book—it's a bridge between timeless wisdom and modern curiosity. With sincerity and clarity, the author guides readers through the symbolic universe of the planets, offering insights that are both deeply personal and universally resonant. A must-read for seekers, scholars, and anyone drawn to the mysteries of the cosmos."

– Rohith

About the Author

Shree Shambav is an internationally acclaimed best-selling author, inspirational speaker, artist, philanthropist, life coach, strategist and entrepreneur. A world record holder, his deep passion for music led him to create soul-stirring albums, drawing inspiration from his celebrated poetry collection, Whispers of Eternity. His profound insights have sparked deep personal transformations, guiding countless individuals toward self-discovery, purposeful living, and authenticity.

With an extraordinary ability to unlock human potential, Shree empowers individuals to break through limitations and embrace their highest selves. His writings, lectures, and compassionate guidance continue to uplift lives, fostering resilience, mindfulness, and personal growth.

Shree Shambav is a 44x best-selling author celebrated for his profound contributions to personal development and spiritual growth.

Shree Shambav's literary journey took flight with the celebrated Journey of Soul - Karma, where he delved into the depths of human experience to unveil profound insights. Garnering recognition through multiple literature awards, his repertoire includes esteemed works, such as the Twenty + One Series, and the enlightening Life Changing Journey – Inspirational Quotes series.

As a distinguished alumnus of the Indian Institute of Management and the National Institute of Technology, Shree Shambav brings a wealth of corporate acumen from his tenure in multinational corporations. His most recent publications, including Unveiling the Enigma, Death - Light of Life and the Shadow of Death and Optimum – Power Python Series I, Series II, Series III and Series IV, demonstrate his mastery of both the literary and technical spheres.

Shree Shambav expands his artistic repertoire with "*Whispers of Eternity: - A Symphony of Soulful Verses*," a heartfelt exploration of the human experience. Alongside this, his "*Whispers of the Soul: A Journey Through Haiku*" distils profound insights into poignant verses. Together, these works showcase his versatility and mastery of soulful expression, inviting readers on a journey of self-discovery. Through his poetry, he weaves a rich tapestry of emotion that resonates deeply with the heart.

Shree Shambav's latest works—*Learn to Love Yourself: A Journey of Discovering Inner Beauty and Strength Through 10 Transformative Rules, The Power of Letting Go: Embrace Freedom and Happiness, A Journey of Lasting Peace—are true treasures of self-discovery, The Entitlement Trap: Get Over It, Get On, Whispers of a Dying Soul: Unspoken Regrets and Unlived Dreams, Whispers of Silence - Unlocking Inner Power through Stillness, The Power of Words: Transforming Speech, Transforming Lives, The Art of Intentional Living: Minimalism for a Life of Purpose, Awakening the Infinite:The Power of Consciousness in Transforming Life, Beyond the Veil: A Journey Through Life After Death series, Bonds Beyond Blood - Where love builds bridges, and bonds defy blood., A Journey into Spiritual Maturity - 12 Golden Rules for Inner Transformation, The Seeker's Gold : Unlocking Life's Greatest Treasure, The Power of Manifestation - Unlocking The Path From Thought To Reality and Born to Rise Series.*

In addition to these works, Shree Shambav has recently ventured into astrology with the release of Astrology Unveiled – Foundations of Ancient Wisdom Series I to VI, expanding into the realm of metaphysics. These books explore the foundational principles of Vedic astrology, offering readers a rich and practical understanding of this ancient wisdom.

Shree Shambav established the Ayur Rakshita Foundation, which is dedicated to promoting boundless growth, universal fraternity, and environmental protection. The charity helps diverse communities while working for societal progress.

To learn more about Shree Shambav and his works, visit his website at www.shambav.org. For information about the Ayur Rakshita Foundation and its initiatives, visit www.shambav-ayurrakshita.org.

Let's Follow him on Social Media: **@shreeshambav**

Main: https://linktr.ee/shreeshambav

Website: https://www.shambav.org/

LinkedIn: https://www.linkedin.com/in/shreeshambav/

Blog: https://blog.shambav.org/

Instagram: https://www.instagram.com/shreeshambav/

YouTube: https://www.youtube.com/@shreeshambav

Amazon: https://www.amazon.com/author/shreeshambav

Goodreads: https://www.goodreads.com/author/show/22367436.Shree_Shambav

PREFACE

This book was not written—it arrived.

It emerged slowly, like the first star in the evening sky—quiet, luminous, and patient. It did not ask to be authored but to be remembered. What lies in these pages is not merely knowledge, but a whisper from something far older than words—a transmission that moves through symbols, silences, shadows, and light.

Over years of contemplation and astrological inquiry, what began as a search for meaning in the dance of planets unfolded into a deeper mystery. I realised I was not studying the cosmos; the cosmos was studying me. Each planetary force, each upagraha, each yantra became less a concept and more a mirror, revealing forgotten dimensions of the self—some bright, some shadowed, all sacred.

This work stands at the confluence of astrology, mysticism, and spiritual vision. It is not meant to predict futures or label lives. Instead, it seeks to reawaken your inner eye to the intelligence of the stars, to the sacred architecture woven into time and space, to the hidden dialogue between your soul and the sky.

The structure of this book mirrors the unfolding of spiritual awareness:

Part One: The Celestial Cabinet opens the veils of the planetary beings—not as cold rocks in the sky, but as luminous archetypes, divine ministers in the vast court of the cosmos, each with a voice and a lesson.

Part Two: The Celestial Order moves deeper into the dance of energy and form, where shadows move with meaning and yantras vibrate with memory. Here, the spiritual geometry of existence begins to reveal itself.

There are deliberate repetitions in these pages, much like the cycles of the moon or the return of Saturn—they are not echoes, but deeper spiral turnings into the same truths. Read slowly. Read aloud, if you can. Let the words enter not only your intellect but your breath, your pulse, your silence.

This book is not an answer. It is a portal.

If it awakens in you a question too large for words, or a memory that cannot be traced, then it has served its purpose.

In gratitude to the stars, the silence, the unseen guides, and the seekers walking this path with open hearts—

I offer this.

With kindest regards,

Shree Shambav

CONTENTS

INTRODUCTION

There are moments in life when time itself seems to pause—when a strange wind whispers across the soul, and one feels that something ancient, immense, and invisible is watching. It is in these moments that we begin to sense the deeper patterns, the quiet architecture of the universe—its silent orbits, its hidden tides, its invisible laws. This book is born from that silence. It is an invitation not to read, but to remember.

Long before telescopes measured distance and algorithms tracked orbits, the sky was our first scripture, and the stars, our earliest teachers. The ancients looked upward—not merely to observe, but to listen. In that celestial listening, they found the voices of the planets, the laughter of constellations, and the firm but gentle guidance of unseen forces. These were not only objects of light, but luminous intelligences—each carrying its own vibration, mystery, and purpose in the evolution of the soul.

Introduction to Planet and The Arrival of Wisdom lay the foundation for this sacred dialogue. They do not merely present astronomy or astrology, but open the door to an inner experience—a space where myth, spirit, and science converge. Here, the planets are not just celestial bodies, but living archetypes. They are both mirrors and masks—reflections of our inner states and catalysts of transformation.

In Part One: The Celestial Cabinet, we enter the inner sanctum where the planetary energies dwell like ancient ministers in the court of the cosmos. Their Mystical Attributes, unveiled in layers, are not descriptions but revelations—poetic impressions of forces that move both the heavens and the human heart.

Part Two: The Celestial Order takes us deeper still, beyond the mythic and into the structural—the rhythms, geometries, and correspondences that bind the seen and the unseen. Here we encounter The Mask and the Mirror, exploring how cosmic forces disguise and reveal the self; we hear The Symphony of Subtle Forces, a music composed in silence; and we learn the Language of Light, the original grammar of creation.

Through Shadows of the Sky and The Dance of Shadows, we come to understand the invisible Upagrahas—forces often omitted, yet silently active in the karma of life. And finally, we bow before the great diagrams of mystery—the Yantras, the sacred geometries of the universe, and the Temples, where stone and spirit meet.

This is not a manual. It is not merely astrology. It is a walk through a sacred grove—where every tree is a planet, every breeze a message, and every shadow a teacher.

May you enter this journey not with the mind of a scholar, but with the heart of a seeker.

Welcome to the dance of the stars.

Warm regards,

Shree Shambav

PROLOGUE

Before the stars were named, before temples were built, before words attempted to explain the heavens, there was a silence.

And in that silence, there was movement.

Not the chaotic motion of things colliding—but a rhythmic unfolding, a dance older than time. This was the birth of cosmic order. From that sacred vibration arose the planets, the nakshatras, the subtle upagrahas, the harmonics of light and shadow. And from that same vibration, the soul began its journey—stepping into time, clothed in form, yet ever longing for the formless.

This book is born from the memory of that original rhythm.

Every civilisation that looked to the sky saw more than stars—they saw messages, patterns, warnings, blessings. They did not separate the heavens from the heart, nor the planets from the personal. They lived in a universe that was not dead matter but living intelligence. For them, Jupiter was not a gas giant—it was Guru, the wisdom giver. Saturn was not a ringed planet—it was Shani, the lord of karmic truth. The upagrahas, often forgotten in modern texts, were known as the subtle agents of shadow work—Maandi, Gulika, Yama Ghantaka—entities not to be feared, but understood and honoured.

What if we, too, could remember that vision?

What if the stars were not distant, but deeply within us? What if every planetary transit were not a force acting upon us, but a signal awakening within us? What if the yantras were not mere diagrams, but the very blueprints of our soul's unfolding?

This book does not aim to teach astrology in the traditional sense. Rather, it offers a pilgrimage through the inner sky—a journey through myth, light, vibration, and the sacred language of the cosmos. It seeks not to calculate, but to evoke. Not to instruct, but to initiate.

You hold in your hands not just a text, but a mirror.

And just beyond this mirror is a door.

To step through it is to enter the temple of the cosmos within you, where planets are not distant bodies, but living archetypes vibrating through your breath, your choices, your fate. You are not separate from this sky—you are its reflection, its echo, its response.

Come. The stars have waited long enough.

Let the journey begin.

Warm regards,

Shree Shambav

Introduction to Planet

"As the celestial dance unfolds above, so too do our lives sway in rhythm below. We are Stardust set in motion, tracing our own constellations across the boundless, ever-shifting sky of existence."— Shree Shambav.

In the magnificent mosaic of ancient Indian astrology, history and the heavens are forever intertwined, echoing one another like twin flames dancing across the fabric of time. Each planetary alignment, each lunar phase, whispers of destinies not yet born and secrets long buried in the scrolls of the universe.

To walk through the corridors of ancient astrology is to step into a sacred dialogue—one between Earth and Sky, between mortal longing and divine orchestration. Here, the stories of kings and queens are not merely historical episodes but celestial dramas played out under the vigilant gaze of the stars. Their horoscopes—etched in time like constellations on parchment—tell of triumph and tragedy, ascension and downfall, love found and kingdoms lost.

These are not tales of myth alone. They are spiritual archetypes, each a mirror reflecting the subtle and profound interconnection between our inner worlds and the greater cosmos. The majestic rise of an emperor, the sorrow of a widow-queen, the valour of a warrior guided by Mars—all emerge as living metaphors, teaching us how the planetary rhythms do not control us, but converse with our consciousness.

Imagine, if you will, a grand celestial loom. Each chapter in this book is a thread—drawn from ancient scripture, royal archives, sacred chants, and oral traditions—woven carefully to recreate a tapestry that reveals not only historical truths but timeless spiritual patterns. Just as the great river Saraswati, though invisible now, continues to nourish India's mystical imagination, so too does the astrological heritage of Bharat continue to irrigate our understanding of fate, free will, karma, and dharma.

These chapters are not academic dissections—they are pilgrimages through a sacred terrain. With reverence, we pause at the junctions where Saturn stood still in the sky before a war was fought. We kneel at the foot of lunar eclipses that changed dynasties. We marvel at birth charts where Jupiter's grace spared a kingdom from ruin.

In delving into these cosmic biographies, we do not merely study astrology; we are initiated into it. We become part of a living tradition that speaks to our desire for meaning, for patterns in the chaos, for the knowledge that our lives are not random acts of chance—but pages in a divine manuscript.

Let these chapters be your lanterns. Let them light the sacred path between the stars and the self. As you turn each page, may you not only discover the power of the planets—but remember that you, too, are made of stardust, woven into the very fabric of this cosmic story.

The Arrival of Wisdom

"The planets do not command us—they invite us. In their silent orbits lie the echoes of choices, the shadows of karma, and the light of awakening." — Shree Shambav

The Arrival of Wisdom – A Morning with Guruji

It was a radiant morning—the kind of morning where even the light felt sacred. The sun stood high above, casting golden beams like blessings upon the earth, as though the heavens themselves leaned a little closer that day. The ashram grounds were abuzz with quiet devotion. Devotees moved like rivers in harmony, flowing between their duties, carrying offerings of love and readiness in their hands and hearts. Their every step echoed an inner mantra, their anticipation building like a sacred hymn, silent yet powerful.

Among them was Abhilasha, her eyes alight with longing—for clarity, for understanding, for divine connection. She meticulously arranged flowers near the Buddha Hall, her fingers trembling not with nervousness, but with reverence. Akanksh moved beside her, whispering soft invocations under her breath, pausing now and then to smile at the morning sun, as if it were an old friend arriving for the same darshan.

Akshatha, grounded and graceful, guided newcomers with calm assurance. Apeksha, curious and reflective, sat beneath a tree with her journal, capturing fleeting insights as they came, hoping they would grow into wisdom. Roopa ensured everything within the hall gleamed—not with perfection, but with love. And then there was Padma, ever watchful, her gaze turning skyward often, seeking alignment not just of stars, but of purpose.

Each of them was a thread, woven into a greater tapestry by the invisible hand of devotion.

As the sun continued its climb, the Buddha Hall, nestled among trees that seemed to bow in silent homage, began to fill. The disciples arrived in waves, not like a crowd, but like a calling. Vasudeva, recited verses under his breath, each word a prayer. Vidyarthi, the young seeker, took his place in the front, eyes wide, soul open. And Aastha, her name itself meaning 'faith,' sat silently with her palms upturned, ready to receive—not just knowledge, but transformation.

And then, without announcement or ceremony, Guruji arrived.

Clad in flowing white robes that caught the sunlight and scattered it gently around him, he seemed not to walk, but to glide—a luminous presence that hushed even the breeze. The air itself shifted. The rustle of robes stilled. Time, it seemed, took a breath.

He entered not like a man, but like the answer to a collective prayer. His presence dissolved the boundaries of individuality, and each person in the room felt not only seen but known—as if their innermost questions had already been heard before they were even spoken.

He offered a simple wave. No words yet, but a current moved through the hall—a current of stillness, of remembrance, of returning home.

With grace that belonged not to performance but to presence, Guruji took his seat. The silence that followed was not empty; it was full—of expectancy, surrender, and love. The disciples adjusted their seats, but no one fidgeted. Even the birds outside seemed to pause.

He raised his hands slowly in Atma Namaste—a gesture of profound reverence. Palms pressed at his heart, head gently bowed. Not just to greet, but to affirm: The divine in me recognises the divine in you.

And in that single, sacred moment, teacher and disciple ceased to be separate. They became one breath, one rhythm, one silence.

Then, in a voice as gentle as morning rain and as powerful as thunder rolling through the soul, Guruji began.

"Indian ancient astrology," he said, "is not merely a tool of prediction. It is the poetry of the cosmos. It is the wisdom of the rishis, written not in ink but in stars. These celestial bodies are not distant spheres—they are reflections of divine will, communicating constantly with the human spirit."

He paused, his gaze resting on Vidyarthi, who leaned in, heart pounding.

"The planets," Guruji continued, "what we call Grahas, are not defined here by astronomical precision. In Vedic astrology, the Sun and Moon are planets—not because of physical structure, but because of their influence. We don't categorize them by what they are, but by what they do. They grasp. They guide. They govern."

His words were not just spoken. They were given—like sacred offerings passed from the soul of the teacher into the hearts of his disciples.

"The Grahas," he said, "are cosmic storytellers. They narrate your karmic imprints, your dharmic pathways. They are not puppeteers but partners. Not fate-writers, but fate-revealers."

A murmur of insight stirred in Padma's heart. She had always feared Saturn—Shani—as a bringer of sorrow. But now, in Guruji's words, she saw him as a stern yet loving teacher, a graha who strips away illusion to lead one to truth.

As the morning ripened into sacred space, Guruji continued—not to lecture, but to awaken. Each sentence was a seed, and in the soil of the disciples' hearts, something eternal began to grow.

In the stillness, in the story, in the stars—the real session had begun.

Illustration sign2: Astrological signs.

Guruji's voice resonated with a profound calm, each word carrying the weight of timeless truth. "In Indian astrology," he began, his tone steeped in awe, "we speak of seven principal Grahas—the Sun, Moon, Mars, Mercury, Jupiter, Venus, and Saturn. They are not merely celestial bodies; they are luminous intelligences, archetypes of energy, messengers of the divine, each with its own rhythm, temperament, and sacred task."

He paused, letting the silence sink in like soft rain into parched soil.

"Imagine, if you will," he continued, "a grand celestial orchestra. The Sun is the conductor, illuminating all, setting the tempo of life, the very pulse of our being. The Moon, gentle and reflective, is the violin, sensitive to every emotional nuance. Mars strikes like a drumbeat of courage and conflict, quick to act. Mercury plays the flute of thought and expression, light, curious, always moving. Jupiter is the cello, deep and wise, resonating with meaning, expansion, and grace. Venus strums the harp of desire, harmony, and love. And Saturn, old and unyielding, plays the gong of time, reminding us of structure, responsibility, and the ultimate lessons we must learn."

The disciples sat, captivated, not merely listening but experiencing—as if their own souls had remembered this song long ago.

Then, Guruji leaned forward, his eyes narrowing with reverent intensity.

"But beyond these, lie the Chaayaa Grahas—Rahu and Ketu—the shadow planets, the unseen players in this orchestra. They are not visible to the eye, for they are not physical in form, but mathematical points where the Sun and Moon's paths intersect, the places where eclipses are born."

Guruji voice lowered to a whisper.

"Rahu, the dragon's head, hungers endlessly for the material, the unfulfilled, the future. It is the illusion, the challenge, the test of ambition without restraint. Ketu, the tail, holds the past, the renunciation, the karmic residue we are here to transcend. Together, they are the guardians of spiritual evolution, tearing down what is false to reveal what is eternal."

As he spoke, Apeksha felt a sudden stirring in her chest—an unspoken memory rising. She had always feared the shadow in her chart. But now, she began to see—Rahu and Ketu weren't punishments. They were spiritual surgeons, slicing away ignorance with surgical precision, so the soul could remember its truth.

Guruji lifted his hand slowly and drew an invisible arc through the air.

"And the story doesn't end there," he said gently. "There are eleven Upagrahas—sub-planets, mathematical echoes that whisper influences of health, temperament, longevity, and spiritual inclination. Though subtle, they are potent—like background instruments in the orchestra, often overlooked, yet capable of shifting the entire melody."

Padma, who had studied texts for years without understanding the Upagrahas' depth, now saw them like gentle breezes influencing the direction of a vast sail—quiet but defining.

Guruji then placed his hand upon his chest.

"And at the heart of it all is the Lagna—the Ascendant—the exact point where the eastern horizon meets the sky at the time of our birth. It is the first breath of the Earth herself in your name, the window through which your soul stepped into the world. It marks the stage from which all the planets perform their roles."

His eyes moistened as he looked upward, the hall silent with reverence.

"This is why we say, astrology is not a tool of fate, but a map of the sacred, a divine design that helps us navigate the terrain of our karmic inheritance and spiritual potential. Every graha, every node, every mathematical whisper in the sky—they are like threads in the loom of the cosmos, weaving the fabric of our existence."

A gentle breeze stirred the curtains of the Buddha Hall, as if the universe had exhaled in agreement.

"Nothing in the chart is accidental," he said. "Every placement, every conjunction, is a signature of the soul's agreement with the cosmos—a reminder that we are not at the mercy of stars, but in dialogue with them."

In that moment, even Rahu and Ketu, so often misunderstood, felt like ancient allies—sacred shadows leading each seeker through the labyrinth of life toward the light of liberation.

Rashi – Sign

Nita's voice rose gently, hesitant yet filled with genuine longing.

"Guruji… what is Rashi?"

She asked not as a student trying to memorize theory, but as a seeker yearning to understand something that had stirred within her for years—a word she had heard often, in family charts and whispered predictions, yet whose essence had remained elusive.

Guruji turned toward her, his gaze softening like the early light of dawn touching the stillness of a temple courtyard. A smile flickered across his lips—not the smile of amusement, but of recognition. He knew the weight of her question. He had once asked it too.

He folded his hands gently in front of him and began to speak—not just with words, but with presence, drawing everyone in like the hush before a sacred ritual.

"Nita," he said, "to understand Rashi, we must first look up—not merely with our eyes, but with the eyes of wonder."

He looked toward the open window, where the sky stretched vast and infinite, as though echoing his words.

Illustration sign3: Astrological signs.

"Imagine the heavens as an enormous celestial canvas," he continued. "The Earth, our sacred blue home, is cradled at the center. From this vantage point, as we observe the sky, we see the planets and stars trace beautiful arcs across this great dome. This apparent path—the ecliptic—is like a celestial river, and it is along this river that the divine players of our lives move, shift, and speak."

He paused for a moment, and all eyes were drawn to the distant sky, now shimmering with soft daylight.

"Now," Guruji said, "this river of the sky—the zodiac—is divided into twelve sacred stretches, each spanning 30 degrees. These are the Rashis. Each Rashi is a field of energy, a temple in the heavens, imbued with qualities, stories, vibrations, and guardianship. They are not merely constellations; they are living archetypes—gateways through which the grahas express themselves."

He turned back to Nita, who now sat breathless, as though a curtain had begun to lift.

"Just as the same drop of rain tastes different depending on where it falls—on stone, in the ocean, in the soil—so too does the energy of a planet express itself uniquely depending on the Rashi it occupies. This positioning is not random; it is precise, calculated in degrees, minutes, and seconds. We call this geocentric measurement the longitude or sphuta of the planet. It tells us not just where the planet is—but how it is singing in the cosmic symphony at that moment."

He walked slowly to a large yantra drawn on the floor—twelve petals encircling a perfect circle.

"This mandala," he said, tracing it with his hand, "is your cosmic fingerprint. Each Rashi is like a house of the soul—a different window through which divine energy shines into your life. For example, Aries—Mesha—is the initiator, the spark, the warrior. Taurus—Vrishabha—is the preserver, the nurturer, the builder. Each Rashi gives color, texture, and personality to the planetary forces."

Nita's eyes filled with tears—not of sorrow, but of recognition.

"Guruji," she whispered, "It's like the planets are artists, and the Rashis are their canvases."

He smiled, deeply pleased.

"Yes. And just as a brushstroke means something different on paper than it does on stone, so too does Mars in Aries act very differently than Mars in Pisces. This is the sacred dance—the merging of motion and meaning."

The disciples sat still, wrapped in the gravity of his words.

Guruji continued, his tone now more meditative:

"In Vedic astrology, we use the Nirayana system—the sidereal zodiac. It aligns the Rashis with the fixed stars, with the ancient rhythm of the cosmos, unshaken by seasons or shifting calendars. It is timeless, like the soul. This differs from the Sayana, or tropical zodiac, used in Western systems, which moves with the equinoxes. Both have their beauty, but ours is the map carved in the stars—unchanging, precise, eternal."

He pointed again to the yantra.

"The full circle is 360 degrees—symbolic of the infinite cycle of time. Each Rashi, each 30-degree segment, is not just a slice of the sky. It is a mirror of the human journey. Twelve Rashis, like twelve pilgrim stations, through which the soul walks, learns, weeps, rejoices, remembers."

Illustration Rashi1: Astrological signs.

He closed his eyes for a moment, his voice now a gentle whisper:

"Nita, Rashi is not just a sign. It is a vessel of karma, dharma, and grace. It is where your story begins. It is where the divine script was first written across the sky."

And in that moment, everyone in the Buddha Hall understood—Rashi was no longer just a term on a chart. It was a window into the sacred, a thread in the tapestry of destiny, a whisper of the divine that said, You belong to the stars—and they to you.

Understanding Rashi and Planetary Placement

Rashi	Sanskrit	Symbol	Start	End
Aries	Mesha	Ar	0°0'0"	29°59'59"
Taurus	Vrishabha	Ta	30°0'0"	59°59'59"
Gemini	Mithuna	Ge	60°0'0"	89°59'59"
Cancer	Karkataka	Cn	90°0'0'	119°59'59"
Leo	Simha	Le	120°0'0"	149°59'59"
Virgo	Kanya	Vi	150°0'0'	179°59'59"
Libra	Thula	Li	180°0'0"	209°59'59"
Scorpio	Vrishcika	Sc	210°0'0"	239°59'59"
Sagittarius	Dhanus	Sg	240°0'0"	269°59'59"
Capricorn	Makara	Cp	270°0'0"	299°59'59"
Aquarius	Kumbha	Aq	300°0'0"	329°59'59"
Pisces	Meena	Pi	360°0'0"	359°59'59"

Illustration Rashi2: Astrological signs.

The zodiac, an immense celestial wheel, spans 360 degrees in total—a sacred circle that captures the eternal rhythm of time and space. This vast continuum is divided into 12 equal segments, each measuring 30 degrees, known as Rashis (zodiac signs). Like twelve divine gates, each Rashi carries a distinct energy, symbolism, and frequency, offering a unique lens through which the planets manifest their influence.

These Rashis form the foundation of Vedic astrology, providing a structured map to decode the ceaseless dance of celestial bodies. Every planet's position within this circle tells a story—a moment in your soul's dialogue with the universe. Understanding where a planet resides is the first step toward understanding how it is shaping your destiny.

Astrological Notation: Decoding Degrees and Rashis

Each planet's position is recorded in zodiacal longitude, a measure that begins at 0° Aries and continues through to 359°59'59"—moving through all twelve Rashis. For example:

When a planet is positioned at 231°40', it lies between 210°00' and 239°59'59", placing it within the Scorpio sign (Rashi 8, Vrischika).

Since each Rashi is 30 degrees, the start of Scorpio (Rashi 8) is at 210°00', and 231°40' means the planet has progressed 21°40' within Scorpio.

This can be expressed as:

21°40' in Sc

21 Sc 40

7s 21°40' (after passing through 7 full signs, the planet has moved 21°40' into the 8th sign, Scorpio).

Each form of notation reflects the same truth—a celestial coordinate full of spiritual meaning.

Exercise 1: Identify the Rashi and Degree Advancement

Use your understanding of zodiacal division to determine the Rashi (zodiac sign) and the degree of advancement of the following planetary positions.

1. Jupiter is located at 174°20'.

Step 1: Divide 174°20' by 30 to find the Rashi. 174° falls in the 6th Rashi (since 6 × 30 = 180, and 174 < 180).

Rashi 6 = Virgo (Kanya)

Degree advancement = 174°20' – 150°00' (start of Virgo) = 24°20'

Answer: Jupiter is at 24°20' in Virgo (24 Kanya 20) or 5s 24°20'

2. Venus is at 5s 17°45'.

"5s" = after passing through 5 full Rashis, i.e., into the 6th Rashi

Rashi 6 = Virgo (Kanya)

Advancement = 17°45' into Virgo

Answer: Venus is at 17°45' in Virgo (17 Kanya 45) or 167°45' in total zodiacal longitude

3. Saturn is positioned at 25 Sa 31.

"25 Sa 31" = 25°31' in Sagittarius (Rashi 9 – Dhanu)

Sagittarius begins at 240°00'

Add: 240° + 25°31' = 265°31' in total zodiacal longitude

Answer: Saturn is at 265°31' total or 25°31' in Sagittarius (25 Dhanu 31) or 8s 25°31'

Exercise 2: Write Your Own Notation

Now it's your turn to create the correct astrological notation from the given longitudes. Practice converting total zodiacal degrees into Rashi placement and degrees within the Rashi.

Questions:

A planet at 95°15’ → What Rashi is this? How far into the Rashi?

A planet at 3s 05°00’ → Convert this to total zodiacal longitude and standard notation.

A planet at 308°20’ → Identify Rashi and degrees into the sign.

Try them yourself before checking the answers!

Between Breaths of Wisdom: The Banyan Tree Break

As the session drew to a pause, Guruji stood, his palms joined in *Atma Namaste.*

Guruji said gently. “Let the teachings breathe. Have your coffee. Let the silence digest the truth.”

The air shifted. And so, they rose.

The Gathering Beneath the Banyan

Under the sprawling **canopy of the banyan**, where golden light dripped like honey through the leaves, the devotees began to gather—**not as students**, but simply as **souls in pause**.

Nita and **Lalitha** were the first to arrive, laughter lingering between them like the last note of a song. **Rohith** followed, cradling his tumbler of steaming filter coffee, the aroma curling upward in holy spirals. **Sujitha** and **Espen** settled on a stone bench nearby, their conversation low and thoughtful—like water flowing over riverstones.

Soon came **Akshaya**, his walk steady, holding a brass cup of chai. Beside him, **Padma** glided like moonlight, her shawl trailing behind her. **Apeksha**, ever observant, held her cup close, as if warming her thoughts before speaking them. **Vasudeva**, with his quiet dignity, offered a nod to each person present—a gesture that felt like a blessing.

The tree watched over them all, its roots like arms, its shade like an embrace.

Moments Between the Teachings

The conversation meandered like a soft stream, winding through reflections of the morning's session.

"What Guruji said about Saturn…" Nita began, "How his abode in hardship reveals the hidden grace in suffering—it stayed with me."

Rohith nodded. "It makes sense now… why the darkest times in life carved the deepest truths in me."

Espen, sipping his chai, added with quiet wonder, "The planets feel like people now. Not distant… not abstract. Like old friends I never learned to greet."

Sujitha, eyes misty, whispered, "I think the Moon lives in me. All this time I thought my sensitivity was a weakness. Today, it felt sacred."

Apeksha smiled but said nothing. She was busy observing—how **Venus glowed in Lalitha's laughter**, how **Mercury played in Espen's insights**, how **Saturn sat quietly in the weariness Vasudeva carried so gracefully**.

Even the coffee cups seemed to carry stories—**the warmth of fire**, the grounding of **earth**, the flow of **water**, the dance of **air**, and the silence of **ether** settling between sips.

The Return Call

The wind stirred the leaves gently, like a reminder that time, too, is a teacher.

Kiran, who had just arrived with an extra cup in hand, stretched and sighed, his voice half a song, half a smile:

"Ah… such stillness. But I think it's time, isn't it? Back to the Buddha Hall. The next wave of wisdom awaits."

Everyone looked up—not with reluctance, but with the kind of peace that comes only after real nourishment. Not just of body… but of soul.

They rose slowly, gathering cups and silence, laughter and lingering thoughts.

The Pause that Breathed

As they walked back toward the hall, the banyan swayed ever so slightly, as if bowing in approval.

And beneath its roots remained the echo of a moment not caught on camera, not written in any book—

but etched into the shared breath of seekers who learned that sometimes, **the holiest teachings are found not in words… but in the spaces between them.**

In chai.

In shadow.

In stillness.

And in **the silence beneath a tree that had watched lifetimes pass.**

Note: Hereafter, Shree Shambav will be referred to as 'Guruji' means Master.

PART ONE

The Celestial Cabinet

"Within every soul is etched a divine signature—

a silent script written by the stars,

revealing not who we are told to be,

but who we were always meant to become."

- *Shree Shambav*

CHAPTER I

The Mystical Attributes I

"To know the stars is not to escape destiny, but to understand its language—so we may walk our path not in fear, but with reverence and purpose." — Shree Shambav

As the Morning light filtered through the sacred lattices of the Buddha Hall, weaving golden patterns across the cool floor, Guruji turned to Akshaya, a young seeker seated with the posture of humility and the fire of inquiry glowing in his eyes. His hands rested in his lap, but his spirit leaned forward—eager, open, and prepared to receive.

Akshaya, unlike many, sought not merely answers, but truth—the kind of truth that dwells behind veils, in the silence between words.

Sensing this deep readiness, Guruji began to speak. His voice moved through the space like a sacred breeze, gentle and profound.

"Akshaya," he said, "in Indian astrology, we begin with a profound act of humility—we place the Earth at the centre of our cosmic understanding. Why? Because astrology is not just a science of space—it is a language of human experience. From where we stand, from our journey on this Earth, we measure the sky and its meanings. And so, we look at the universe not from the outside in, but from the inside out."

He paused, letting the gravity of those words settle in the hearts of all present.

"From this sacred vantage point, the planets appear to revolve around us. In the outer circle move the majestic giants—Mars, the warrior; Jupiter, the teacher; Saturn, the judge of time. In the inner circle, closer to Earth, journey Venus, the harmoniser; Mercury, the thinker; and the Sun, the sovereign soul. Then, more intimately, we consider the Moon, the luminous mirror of our emotions—and the subtle forces of Rahu and Ketu, the shadow points that bind our karmic threads."

Guruji now gestured to a drawn yantra on the floor—a concentric mandala of planetary orbits.

"These movements are not just motions in space," he said. "They are movements within us. What happens in the sky stirs echoes in the soul. The Moon, dearest disciples, orbits Earth at a slight tilt—crossing the Sun's path at two critical points. These crossing points are Rahu and Ketu—not visible planets, but powerful intersections of fate. One draws us forward into our desires, our attachments. The other pulls us back, toward detachment, toward wisdom earned in prior lives."

Akanksh, seated nearby, shifted slightly, absorbing the revelation with a steady gaze. These weren't abstract symbols anymore. They were forces he could feel in his own unfolding life.

Then Akshaya asked, his voice low but firm with intent,

"Guruji, what does it mean when we say 'Lord' in astrology?"

Guruji smiled. It was a smile like the quiet before a monsoon—a prelude to something nourishing and deep.

"Ah," he said, "an important question indeed. In Vedic astrology, the word 'Lord'—or Swami—means 'Master' or 'Ruler.' Every Rashi, every zodiac sign, has a ruling planet. And when a sign occupies a house in your chart, its ruler becomes the Lord of that house."

He turned the yantra around and drew—a kundali, the birth chart.

"Each of these twelve houses is like a room in the palace of your life. One speaks of your body, another of your family, another of your speech, another of your karma. Each house has a gatekeeper, a ruling energy that manages its affairs. This gatekeeper—the planetary Lord—determines how the room feels, how its energies are accessed, whether it flows with ease or with resistance."

Akshaya leaned in closer, his breath quiet, his awareness sharp.

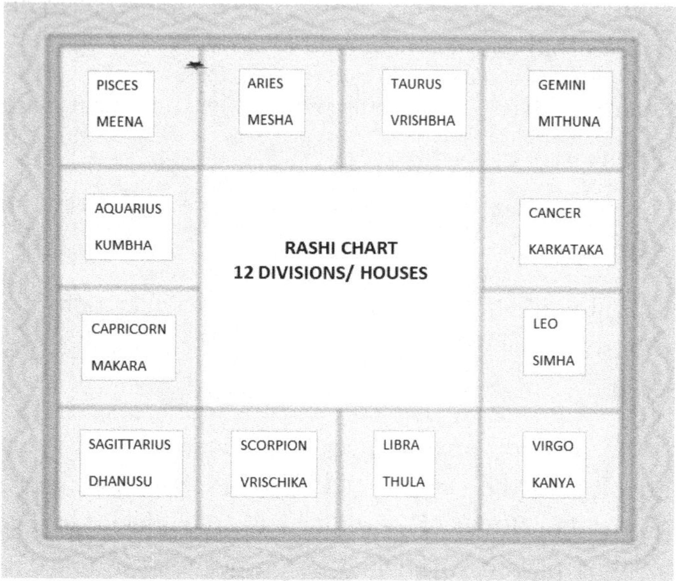

Illustration Div1: 12 Divisions or Houses

"For instance," Guruji continued, "if the first house in your chart is Aries, its Lord is Mars. Mars, then, becomes the protector and commander of your physical vitality, your will, your identity. If Mars is strong, your confidence will be bold and assertive. If Mars is weakened or afflicted, your drive may falter, or become misdirected. It is like a ruler who governs a kingdom—not to control, but to guide. The state of the ruler affects the fate of the realm."

He looked now at Akanksh, who had once struggled to understand the shifting winds of his career.

"Similarly," Guruji said, "if the tenth house—the house of career—is ruled by Saturn, and Saturn is in a strong position, your path will be one of discipline, endurance, and eventual recognition. If Saturn is weak or burdened, you may face delays, but even those delays will become part of your learning."

He paused, then added with emphasis:

"The Lords in your chart are not distant deities. They are aspects of your inner being, the very energies you chose before you took birth. They are your karmic guides. Not fate-bringers, but fate-revealers."

A long silence followed. Not because there was nothing left to say, but because the words had reached their mark. Both Akshaya and Akanksh sat transformed—no longer seeking merely to understand astrology, but to understand themselves through it.

The Rashi Chakra: The Divine Wheel of Time

Birds chirped gently in the nearby trees, as if offering their hymns to the sacred silence within. The air was crisp, touched with the scent of sandalwood incense rising in lazy spirals toward the rafters.

The disciples sat in quiet reverence. Among them was Akshaya, seated with calm alertness, his palms resting on his knees, his eyes reflecting the quiet flame of inquiry that burned deep within.

Guruji, seated before the mandala of planetary symbols on the floor, exhaled a breath that seemed to dissolve into the very air around him. He looked at Akshaya, then gently raised his hand toward the light pouring in through the eastern archway.

"Akshaya," he said, his voice like a mantra wrapped in wind, "the zodiac is more than a map of stars—it is the breath of Time itself, flowing through the heavens. In Sanskrit, we call it the Rashi Chakra or Kala Chakra—the wheel of divine time, forever turning, forever guiding."

He gestured slowly toward the eastern horizon visible through the trees.

"The zodiac is a sacred belt in the sky—about 8 degrees above and below the ecliptic, the apparent path the Sun traces across the celestial sphere throughout the year. But this belt is not exclusive to the Sun. The Moon, too, dances within it. The planets—our celestial teachers—journey along it. Together, they trace stories across the heavens that mirror the inner unfolding of our souls."

The disciples listened with rapt stillness, their breaths in unison with the rhythm of his words.

"This 360-degree circle is divided into twelve Rashis, twelve signs of the zodiac. Each spans 30 degrees, each one a cosmic archetype, a divine doorway through which planetary energies enter our lives. But beneath the Rashis lie more ancient stars—the 27 Nakshatras, the Moon's mansions. These are not just constellations; they are soul imprints, each imbued with unique qualities, ruling deities, and mythic stories."

Guruji walked slowly to a yantra on the floor—a wheel segmented with sacred geometry.

"Each Nakshatra is further divided into four padas, or quarters. These divisions are not just technical—they are the subtle notes in the celestial song. Every Rashi holds nine padas, and each pada, just 3 degrees and 20 minutes, is like a heartbeat in the rhythm of the cosmos."

He looked back at Akshaya, whose face now bore the quiet shine of insight dawning.

"The planets, Akshaya, are not floating stones in the sky. They are living forces, embodiments of divine will. They do not just move through space—they move through you. The Sun and Moon each govern one sign—Leo and Cancer, respectively. The others hold rulership over two signs each: Mars over Aries and Scorpio, Venus over Taurus and Libra, Mercury over Gemini and Virgo, Jupiter over Sagittarius and Pisces, and Saturn over Capricorn and Aquarius."

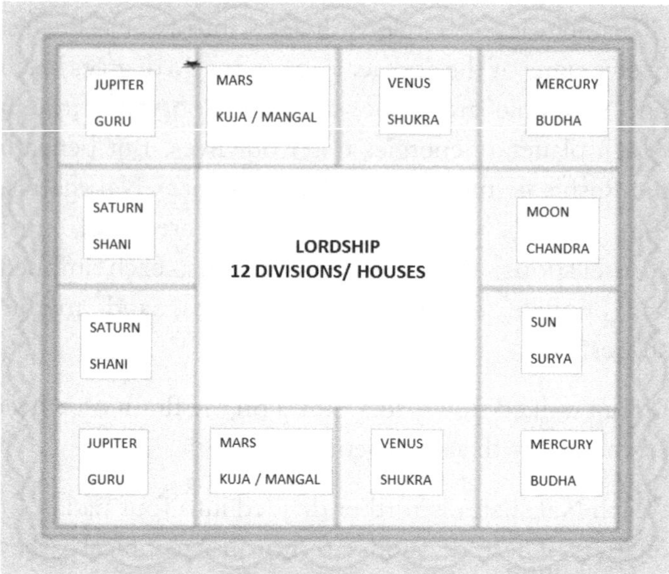

Illustration Lord1: Lordship of Divisions or Houses

He paused, the sacred geometry at his feet glowing in the morning light.

"And then come Rahu and Ketu—the shadows. They have no physical bodies, yet they shape destinies. Born from the intersection of the Earth's orbit around the Sun and the Moon's orbit around Earth, these are the north and south lunar nodes. They are not seen—but they are deeply felt. Rahu, the head of the dragon, pulls us forward into desires, lessons not yet learned. Ketu, the tail, draws us backward into detachment and remembrance."

The air in the hall was now imbued with stillness—not of emptiness, but of presence.

"The Rashis, Akshaya, represent the ever-changing costumes worn by consciousness in its journey through life. They are the stages of evolution, the fields in which karma is sown and harvested. The planets are like divine actors, and your birth chart is their script, their sacred stage. But remember—you are not the chart. You are the soul behind the story."

Then, with profound gentleness, Guruji concluded:

"Just as Lord Vishnu manifests through various incarnations, the zodiac is His form in time and space. The Rashis are His limbs. The planets are His messengers. The Nakshatras are His voice. To study astrology is not just to study fate—it is to read the divine blueprint, to remember that life is not random but woven with sacred design."

As the morning sun climbed a little higher, casting a soft glow on every disciple's face, Akshaya closed his eyes—not in retreat, but in deep recognition. The sky was no longer far above. It was within.

And thus, as another day of wisdom began, the great wheel of time turned once more, silently whispering the eternal truth: "As above, so within."

Characteristics of Planets

C1: The Planets as Divine Avatars: A Sacred Unfolding of Essence

Guruji's voice was gentle but firm, like the river that cuts stone not by force, but by constancy.

"In the cosmic design," he began, "there are two fundamental energies from which all beings are born—Paramaatmaamsa, the supreme divine essence, and Jeevaamsa, the individual soul essence, or life force."

He closed his eyes briefly, and it seemed the whole hall grew quieter in response.

"The planets, or Grahas, are not mere astronomical entities—they are luminous deities, carriers of divine will. Each one is a mirror, a doorway, through which a portion of that infinite divine intelligence expresses itself. And in this sacred interplay of energies, the avatars of the Supreme take form—not randomly, but in correspondence with the planets' archetypal nature."

Guruji slowly rose, moving toward a large circular yantra that bore the names and symbols of the nine grahas. With each step, his words deepened:

The Sacred Mapping of Avatars to Planets

"Each planet," he said, "is a reflection of a specific vibration of consciousness—a unique flavour of divine intervention meant to restore balance, guide souls, and reawaken the eternal truth. Let me show you."

He raised his hand toward the shadowy, mysterious Ketu, its symbol subtle, like the end of a breath.

Planet	Avatar	Name Variants	Symbolism
Ketu	Fish Avatar	Meena / Matsya	Cosmic salvation through the shadow planet
Saturn	Tortoise Avatar	Koorma	Patience and resilience
Rahu	Hog Avatar	Varaha / Sookara	Restoration of order amidst chaos
Mars	Half-Lion, Half-Man Avatar	Narasimha / Nrisimha	Raw power and protection
Jupiter	Dwarf Avatar	Vaamana	Wisdom and humility
Venus	Warrior Sage Avatar	Parashurama / Bhaargava Rama	Discipline and retribution
Sun	Prince Avatar	Rama	Righteousness and dharma
Moon	Divine Lover Avatar	Krishna	Divine love, joy, and transcendence
Mercury	Enlightened Avatar	Buddha	Enlightenment and intellectual clarity

Illustration C1: Characteristics of Planets

"From Ketu, the south node, arises Matsya, the Fish Avatar. Just as the fish swims in the primordial ocean of chaos, Ketu guides us through dissolution, into moksha—liberation. It is the energy of salvation, surrender, and transcendence. Ketu appears when the known world begins to fade, and only trust remains."

Then, to Saturn, marked by its heavy, solemn glyph.

"From Saturn comes Koorma, the Tortoise Avatar. This is the embodiment of endurance. When the gods and demons churned the cosmic ocean, it was Koorma who bore the mountain on his back—just as Saturn teaches us to carry the weight of karma, with patience and perseverance. His lessons are slow, but his rewards are eternal."

He turned next to Rahu, the north node, shrouded in curiosity and chaos.

"Rahu gives rise to Varaha, the Boar Avatar—the one who dives into the mud of maya to retrieve the sacred Earth. Rahu represents illusion, hunger, and the quest for purpose. But even in the chaos, the divine descends—reminding us that truth can be reclaimed even in the most distorted of realms."

Now to Mars, fiery and bold.

"From Mars, we receive Narasimha, the Half-Lion, Half-Man Avatar—the divine protector who emerges from a pillar of certainty and surprise, to destroy the tyrant of ego. Mars is courage, righteous anger, divine protection—he teaches us that sometimes, fierce compassion must rise to defend dharma."

Guruji's voice softened as he pointed to Jupiter, glowing in yellow and gold.

"From Jupiter, comes Vaamana, the Dwarf Avatar, small in stature but vast in wisdom. Jupiter is the Guru of the cosmos, the bringer of insight, expansion, and divine understanding. Vaamana teaches that humility can encompass the universe when rooted in wisdom."

He now gestured to Venus, radiant and serene.

"Parashurama, the warrior sage, is born of Venus. This might seem surprising—Venus, the planet of beauty and pleasure—yet Venus also governs devotion and purification. Parashurama's axe is not for destruction alone—it is to cut through ignorance, to protect purity and spiritual integrity."

Next came the Sun, glowing at the centre of the yantra like the soul itself.

"From Surya, the Sun, arises Sri Rama, the embodiment of Dharma. The Sun is our inner king, our clarity, our truth, our unwavering sense of right action. Rama's life is the ideal journey of duty and sacrifice, and the Sun teaches us how to shine, not for the self, but for all."

He turned toward the Moon, cool and gentle.

"From Chandra, the Moon, emerges Krishna, the cosmic lover, the flute-player of eternity. Where the Sun is the father, the Moon is the mother—nurturing, artistic, playful, wise beyond words. Krishna teaches us that life is a dance, that joy and devotion are not distractions, but sacred paths."

Finally, Guruji pointed to Mercury, swift and clever.

"From Budha, Mercury, comes the Buddha—the one who awakens, who sees through illusion. Mercury governs intellect, speech, and discernment. In his higher form, he becomes the embodiment of enlightenment, the cool clarity that pierces through confusion."

The Divine Ratio: Paramaatmaamsa and Jeevaamsa

Guruji turned back to face the disciples, who sat in silent awe.

"These Avatars, Akshaya," he said softly, "are not like us. They are born with a higher proportion of Paramaatmaamsa—the supreme essence. That's what makes them divine. We, too, carry that essence, but mixed with Jeevaamsa—the soul's evolving spark, subject to karma and rebirth. The planets guide us by awakening their unique essence within us. We may not be Rama or Krishna—but their light lives within us, waiting to be remembered."

He gestured to each disciple as if addressing their very core:

"When you feel the weight of Saturn, think of Koorma. When lost in desire, remember Rahu's Varaha. When you're called to protect the truth, invoke Narasimha. The Avatars are not distant myths—they are energies waiting to awaken in your chart, in your life, in your very breath."

And with that, Guruji folded his hands in Atma Namaste, as if bowing not to his disciples—but to the divine spark within each of them.

C2: Benefics and Malefics: The Guiding Forces of Karma

Guruji said, "Every planet, whether considered benefic or malefic, is ultimately a teacher of the soul. Some teach through blessings, others through trials—but all serve the evolution of consciousness."

In Vedic astrology, the nine planetary forces (Navagrahas) are broadly classified into natural benefics (Saumya or Subha Grahas) and natural malefics (Kroora or Paapa Grahas). This classification helps us understand their inherent tendencies—whether they are naturally inclined to bestow harmony and growth, or to bring challenges and transformation.

Category	Planets	Notes / Conditions
Natural Benefics	Jupiter, Venus, Mercury (if unaffiliated or with benefics), Waxing Moon	Saumya Grahas or Subha Grahas. Promote positivity, good fortune, and growth.
Natural Malefics	Sun, Mars, Rahu, Ketu, Mercury (if with malefics), Waning Moon	Known as Kroora Grahas or Paapa Grahas. Bring obstacles, challenges, and hardships.

Illustration C2: Characteristics of Planets

Natural Benefics (Saumya/Subha Grahas)

Jupiter (Guru) and Venus (Shukra) are the most auspicious planets in the celestial family. They are inherently generous, life-giving, and expansive in their influence. Jupiter represents wisdom, dharma, and spiritual guidance. Venus governs love, beauty, and comfort. Together, they embody divine grace and inner harmony.

Mercury (Budha) is considered a neutral planet, but when unafflicted and accompanied by other benefics, it functions as a natural benefic. In such a state, it promotes intelligence, communication, and adaptability with clarity and balance.

The Moon, when waxing (moving from New Moon to Full Moon—Shukla Paksha), is also treated as a benefic. A waxing Moon represents growth, nurturing, and emotional prosperity, often bringing comfort, support, and peace of mind.

These benefic planets, when well-placed in a natal chart, tend to bestow favourable results—including emotional well-being, financial growth, strong relationships, and spiritual blessings.

Natural Malefics (Kroora/Paapa Grahas)

The Sun (Surya), Mars (Mangala), Rahu, and Ketu are considered natural malefics, though not inherently "bad." Their role is to challenge, provoke, purify, and accelerate karmic learning.

The Sun, though the soul and source of life, is also a force of heat, ego, and intensity. When afflicted, it can burn away balance and invite pride or isolation.

Mars is a warrior—disciplined and protective, yet prone to aggression when imbalanced.

Rahu, the north node, represents obsession, illusion, and insatiable desire, while Ketu, the south node, symbolises detachment, past karma, and spiritual disconnection.

Mercury, when conjoined with malefics, adopts their qualities, becoming a functional malefic. Its neutrality makes it easily influenced, and its results depend heavily on the company it keeps.

The Moon, when waning (from Full Moon to New Moon—Krishna Paksha), is also viewed as malefic. A waning Moon may bring emotional instability, confusion, or detachment from nourishing energies.

Malefic planets, while more likely to introduce struggles or setbacks, are not adversaries—they are catalysts. They invoke strength, discipline, and transformation, often compelling the individual to grow beyond their comfort zone and into greater self-awareness.

A Sacred Balance

Understanding the nature of benefics and malefics is essential in chart interpretation, as their influence shapes the tone of life experiences, from the smooth to the turbulent.

Guruji said:

"No planet is your enemy. Even Rahu, who distorts, and Saturn, who delays, are not there to punish—but to polish the soul. The malefics train you in courage. The benefics remind you of grace. Together, they form the divine rhythm of your karma."

Ultimately, it is not just the classification, but the placement, aspects, dignity, and house rulerships that determine how a planet will act in your chart. With awareness, even a malefic becomes a friend, and even a benefic becomes a guide—each carrying you forward on the journey of self-realisation.

The Divine Ministers of Human Destiny: A Cosmic Story of Planetary Governance

Inside, there was a stillness that only the morning knows—a silence not of absence, but of presence, as if even the air had paused to listen.

Sam sat in silence, his eyes fixed on Guruji, who stood beside a great mural of the solar system. But it wasn't just a diagram of planets and orbits—it was a cosmic mandala, an expression of divine intelligence in motion.

Guruji said, "In the kingdom of life," he began, "there are divine ministers appointed by the Supreme—each entrusted with the care of a particular realm of your existence. These are the Navagrahas, the nine planetary governors of your soul's journey through time."

He raised his hand and pointed to the golden symbol of the Sun, glowing at the centre.

The Sun – King of the Cosmos, Lord of the Soul (Atma)

"The Sun, or Surya, is the sovereign ruler—the emperor of your celestial kingdom. He governs your Atma, your core essence, the spark that remains untouched even in a thousand lifetimes. The Sun is your purpose, your light, your dharma. When he shines bright in your chart, you walk with clarity, with noble vision, and with the confidence of someone who knows they are guided by inner truth."

Guruji paused and added,

"But beware—the same Sun that illuminates can burn, if not tempered by humility. The Sun teaches us to lead not with ego, but with grace."

Category	Planets	Notes / Conditions
Natural Benefics	Jupiter, Venus, Mercury (if unaffiliated or with benefics), Waxing Moon	Saumya Grahas or Subha Grahas. Promote positivity, good fortune, and growth.
Natural Malefics	Sun, Mars, Rahu, Ketu, Mercury (if with malefics), Waning Moon	Known as Kroora Grahas or Paapa Grahas. Bring obstacles, challenges, and hardships.

Illustration C3: Characteristics of Planets

The Moon – Queen of Emotion, Ruler of the Mind (Manas)

"The Moon, or Chandra, is the Queen, the ruler of the Manas, or mind—but not just intellect. The Moon governs your feelings, your moods, and your intuitive whispers. She is the gentle hand on your forehead, the tide that pulls your memories to the surface. She doesn't command—she reflects, and in doing so, reveals your emotional truth."

He looked at Sam and said gently,

"A calm Moon brings peace. A troubled Moon, and the entire kingdom trembles."

Mars – The Commander, Guardian of Power and Courage

"Mars, or Mangala, is the warrior, the protector. He rules over your physical energy, your willpower, and your ability to take action. Think of him as the general at the gates—fierce, decisive, and alert. He gives you the fire to fight for what is right, and the courage to face your own fears."

Guruji raised an eyebrow.

"But a wounded Mars becomes anger, aggression, and restlessness. He must be trained—like a sword in the hands of a yogi."

Mercury – The Messenger, Lord of Speech and Thought

"Mercury, or Budha, is the scribe of the cosmos—the one who writes your thoughts, shapes your speech, and guides your learning. He governs communication, reason, adaptability, and youthful curiosity."

Guruji smiled.

"When Mercury is awake in you, your words heal, your ideas flow, and your intellect dances like a river. But if clouded, he brings confusion, miscommunication, and anxiety."

Jupiter – The Guru, Bringer of Wisdom and Expansion

"Jupiter, or Guru, is your inner teacher. He rules over your wisdom, your values, your capacity to forgive, to hope, to believe. Jupiter doesn't just guide—it blesses. He expands whatever he touches—your knowledge, your family, your faith."

Guruji placed his hand on his heart.

"He is the voice of your conscience, the one who reminds you that there is a higher purpose in everything you face."

Venus – The Artist, Guardian of Love and Beauty

"Venus, or Shukra, is the lover, the poet, the artist. He rules your pleasure, romance, creativity, and aesthetic sense. Venus teaches you to experience life as a work of art, to find beauty in the mundane, to love deeply, and to create joyfully."

He added,

"But if indulged too much, Venus can lead you into illusion—mistaking comfort for fulfilment."

Saturn – The Judge, Keeper of Time and Karma

"Ah… Saturn, or Shani, the most misunderstood of all," Guruji said with deep reverence.

"Saturn governs grief, structure, responsibility, and karma. He is the timekeeper, slow and steady, teaching through patience and delay. His lessons often come wrapped in suffering, but inside are the seeds of your greatest strength."

Guruji closed his eyes briefly.

"He teaches you what cannot be learned in comfort."

Planetary Colours: The Sacred Spectrum of Consciousness

Guruji then moved toward a tray of colored cloths laid out on the altar.

"Each planet radiates a vibration, and that vibration resonates as colour. These hues are not just symbolic—they reflect the planet's essence, and they subtly influence our choices, preferences, and even our state of mind."

He held up each cloth, one by one:

Planet	Colour	Symbolism
Sun	Blood-Red / Saffron	Vitality, energy, life force
Moon	Tawny	Gentleness, nurturing, emotional influence
Mars	Blood-Red	Fire, assertiveness, action-oriented nature
Mercury	Grass-Green	Intellect, communication, adaptability
Jupiter	Tawny / Yellow	Wisdom, growth, expansiveness
Venus	Multiple Colours / White	Beauty, love, harmony
Saturn	Black	Discipline, seriousness, karmic influence

Illustration C4: Characteristics of Planets

Sun – Blood red / Saffron: the energy of vitality, leadership, and life force.

Moon – Pale tawny: the colour of empathy, reflection, and calm.

Mars – Bright red: symbolising assertiveness, passion, and drive.

Mercury – Grass green: representing intellect, clarity, and adaptability.

Jupiter – Yellow or tawny: the light of wisdom, generosity, and expansion.

Venus – White or multicoloured: the spectrum of beauty, harmony, and desire.

Saturn – Deep black: the hue of depth, maturity, and karmic purification.

"When choosing personal items," he said, "such as clothing, accessories, or even the colour of your vehicle—tune in. Aligning with your planetary energies through colour is a way of honouring the cosmic forces within and around you."

The Cosmic Orchestra

Guruji stepped back and looked upon his disciples with love.

"Remember, every planet plays a unique instrument in the orchestra of your soul. The Sun is your drumbeat of purpose, the Moon your lyre of emotion, Mercury your flute of expression, and so on. When in harmony, you become a symphony—a moving, breathing expression of the Divine."

And as the morning breeze stirred the bells at the entrance of the hall, a silence full of meaning descended once again.

The Celestial Court: Planetary Deities and the Divine Cabinet of the Cosmos

Roopa, after a pause, asked, "Guruji, about the deities behind the planets—not merely the astronomical or astrological significance, but the divine intelligence animating each graha."

Guruji opened his eyes, his expression serene, his voice a soft chord of sunrise:

"Roopa, the planets are not just forces. They are beings—conscious, radiant emissaries of Divine Will. In the sacred Vedic vision, they form the Cosmic Cabinet, each assigned a celestial role, each governed by a deity who reflects their deepest essence."

Planet	Role in Cosmic Cabinet	Symbolism
Sun	King	Authority, power, soul
Moon	Queen	Emotions, mind, nurturing energy
Mars	Commander-in-Chief	Strength, courage, military force
Mercury	Prince	Intellect, communication, adaptability
Jupiter	Minister of Wisdom	Knowledge, righteousness, spiritual guidance
Venus	Minister of Beauty	Love, beauty, harmony, pleasures
Saturn	Servant	Discipline, hard work, service

Illustration C5: Characteristics of Planets

He moved to a large tapestry hanging behind him—a divine council, embroidered in golden thread: planets adorned with crowns, halos, and weapons, seated in a court that mirrored heaven itself.

The Sun – The King (Surya), Deity: Agni

"The Sun, Roopa," he said, "is the King of the Cosmic Court—majestic, central, sovereign. His deity is Agni, the god of fire, the carrier of prayers, the essence of vitality and transformation. Just as a king offers vision, order, and radiance, so too does Surya bestow purpose and clarity. He illuminates the path of the soul (Atma).

He does not beg—he commands. His fire is not cruel, but purifying, demanding that we burn away ego and walk in dharma."

Guruji's gaze grew intense, as if calling forth the Sun itself.

"To ignore the Sun in your chart is to ignore the voice of your higher self."

Planet	Presiding Deity	Symbolism and Qualities
Sun	Agni (God of Fire)	Vitality, authority, illumination
Moon	Chandra / Soma	Reflective light, soothing energy, emotional depth
Mars	Subrahmanya / Kartikeya	Courage, action, determination, leadership
Jupiter	Maha Vishnu	Wisdom, expansion, protection, benevolence
Venus	Sachi Devi (Consort of Indra)	Beauty, love, grace, harmony
Saturn	Brahma (Creator)	Discipline, structure, time, karmic lessons

Illustration C6: Characteristics of Planets

The Moon–The Queen (Chandra), Deity: Soma

"And the Moon, our Queen," he continued, his tone softening, "ruled by Chandra, or Soma, is the gentle mirror of divine feeling. She does not shine her own light but reflects the King's radiance with compassion. Where the Sun gives purpose, the Moon gives meaning. She is emotion, intuition, memory—the womb of our inner world."

He turned to Roopa.

"A mother's love, a lover's touch, a poet's tears—these all belong to the Moon."

Mars–Commander-in-Chief (Mangala), Deity: Subrahmanya/Kartikeya

"Mars is the Commander, the enforcer of the King's will, the one who rides into battle with sword in hand. His deity is Subrahmanya—also known as Kartikeya, the divine warrior born of Shiva's flame. He embodies valor, courage, and strategy."

Guruji raised his hand in a firm gesture.

"When you need to protect your truth, break inertia, or rise after a fall, call upon Mars. But remember—this commander fights only for dharma. Misused, his fire turns to rage. Honored, he becomes your strength."

Mercury–The Prince (Budha), Deity: Vishnu's Aspect

"Mercury, the Prince, is youthful, curious, and brilliant. He is the playful diplomat of the planetary court, ruled by an aspect of Vishnu—the divine preserver. Budha governs communication, intelligence, humor, and wit."

He smiled gently.

"Like a clever prince navigating palace politics, Mercury adapts and learns quickly. He reflects the voice of your mind—whether it whispers poetry or spins confusion depends on how aligned he is with your higher truth."

Jupiter–The Guru/Minister (Brihaspati), Deity: Maha Vishnu

"Ah, Jupiter," Guruji said, his voice tinged with reverence, "is the chief minister, the Guru. His deity is Maha Vishnu, the Supreme Preserver, the one who expands, protects, and sustains the universe."

He pressed his palm to his heart.

"Jupiter is the guardian of truth, faith, and knowledge. He teaches that growth without wisdom is illusion. When he blesses, he gives in abundance—children, joy, dharma, purpose. But even his absence is a lesson in humility."

Venus–The Minister of Grace (Shukra), Deity: Sachi Devi

"Venus is the minister of pleasure, art, and beauty. Her deity is Sachi Devi, the consort of Indra, representing grace, sensuality, and divine harmony. Where Jupiter is the guide of sacred truth, Venus is the guide of sacred pleasure. Both are essential. Without beauty, the truth is dry. Without wisdom, beauty is empty."

Guruji held up a delicate lotus petal.

"Venus teaches you how to love, to create, to rejoice—but always with alignment. When love becomes indulgence, she withdraws her light."

Saturn–The Servant (Shani), Deity: Brahma

"And now, Saturn," Guruji said, his voice now heavier, filled with solemnity.

"Saturn is the Servant, but make no mistake—his role is not lowly. His deity is Brahma, the creator, the architect of time and form. Saturn teaches through delay, repetition, endurance. He builds your character in silence, often through hardship."

Guruji's eyes shimmered with compassion.

"If you feel forgotten, left behind, tested again and again—it is Saturn's school. And if you stay long enough, he gives what no one else can: mastery."

Rahu and Ketu–The Shadow Army, Karmic Catalysts

"And finally, Rahu and Ketu," he said, turning to the two shadowy symbols embroidered in silver thread. "They are not part of the royal court, but they form the invisible army—forces of transformation, karma, illusion, and awakening."

"Rahu is the tempter, the foreigner, the outcast who shows you what you secretly crave. Ketu is the renunciate, the mystic who cuts you free from what no longer serves you. They answer to no deity, yet all deities work through them, for they bring your karma to the surface."

Guruji closed his eyes for a moment, then opened them again, shining with ancient remembrance.

"Each of these planets is a living archetype, a deity in motion. When you honor their lessons, you are not surrendering to fate—you are learning to dance with the divine. The planets are not just 'out there'—they are alive within you, governing your thoughts, your actions, your dharma."

Gender Association of Planets: A Sacred Glimpse into Creation

Abhilasha, seated near the front, raised her hand slowly and asked with quiet reverence, "Guruji, can the stars reveal the nature of a soul yet to come? Can we know if the child will be a boy or a girl?"

A knowing smile formed on Guruji's lips, not of arrogance, but of compassionate understanding. He closed his eyes for a brief moment—perhaps listening to a language that only the inner ear could hear.

"Ah, Abhilasha," he began, "the womb of destiny is sacred. Just as a potter molds clay but cannot always see the final form until the wheel stops, so too do we approach the mystery of birth with humility and reverence. Still, the stars offer hints, signs that whisper the possibilities. For those who listen, there is guidance."

Planet	Gender Classification	Implications
Jupiter	Male	Often associated with male offspring and masculine traits
Mars	Male	Signifies male energy, assertiveness, and physical vitality
Sun	Male	Represents masculine authority, leadership, and strength
Venus	Female	Associated with female offspring, love, and beauty
Moon	Female	Linked with femininity, nurturing, and emotional sensitivity
Mercury	Neutral/Variable	Exhibits both male and female traits depending on context
Saturn	Neutral/Variable	Tends toward femininity in certain interpretations

Illustration C7: Characteristics of Planets

The Masculine, Feminine, and Neutral Forces in the Sky

"In Vedic astrology," Guruji continued, "planets are imbued with gendered energies—not as rigid biological roles, but as expressions of polarity and archetype. These energies influence how life unfolds, including the potential gender of offspring, when the conditions are ripe for conception."

Masculine Planets:

Jupiter, the wise Guru—representing divine will, lineage, and progeny.

Mars, the fiery warrior—symbolising strength, virility, and assertive life force.

The Sun, radiant king—associated with the soul, dominance, and masculine essence.

Feminine Planets:

Venus, the goddess of love—reflecting nurturing, creativity, and feminine grace.

The Moon, the mother of the night—embodying emotion, fertility, and receptivity.

Neutral Planets (Context-Dependent):

Mercury, the youthful communicator—adaptive, mutable, can mirror the qualities of accompanying planets.

Saturn, the elder of karma—often regarded as neutral but can lean toward the feminine in certain chart dynamics due to its receptive, restrictive nature.

"These gendered energies become significant," Guruji said, "especially when we analyze the 5th house—the house of children, of creation, and of joy."

Story Example: A Chart Reveals Its Whisper

Guruji touched the 5th house, marked by auspicious signs and planetary symbols.

"Let us walk together through an example. This is the natal chart of a young couple seeking insight into their future child."

Chart Details:

Jupiter is prominently placed in the 5th house, strong in its own sign.

Mars is also conjunct Jupiter in the 5th house.

Mercury sits in the 7th house but casts a strong drishti (aspect) on the 5th house.

The Moon is in the 9th house, distant, with no aspect on the 5th.

Venus rests quietly in the 10th house, with no angular influence on the house of children.

Guruji gently tapped the chart.

"See here," he said, "this house of children is filled with the fiery brilliance of Jupiter and Mars—both masculine, potent planets. They are not only present, but in dignity, giving their full influence. Mercury, though neutral, leans masculine here, because of his proximity to Mars in energy and aspect."

He motioned toward the other side of the chart.

"The Moon and Venus, the gentle matriarchs of the cosmos, are absent from this house. They offer no nurturing influence here, no softening rays of feminine energy."

Guruji's eyes softened, and his voice dropped to a whisper.

"From this alignment, I spoke to the couple—not with certainty, for only God knows—but with respectful clarity. I said, 'If the soul arrives under these skies, it may most likely be a boy, carrying the lineage of fire and wisdom. But remember, the child's gender is only the outer garment. What truly matters is the quality of soul that enters your life.'"

He looked back at Abhilasha and the others.

"In the end, the couple gave birth to a son, a child with bright eyes and a steady gaze. Years later, they returned, smiling, saying the boy showed signs of Jupiter even at the age of six—wise beyond his years, constantly asking, 'What is truth?"'

Conclusion: The Child as a Cosmic Guest

"Abhilasha," Guruji said with warmth, "when we try to determine the gender of a child through the chart, we are not trying to define the child—but to prepare for their arrival. It is like reading the wind before a guest arrives—will they bring the fire of the Sun or the fragrance of the Moon?"

"The chart shows us the gate through which the soul may enter. Masculine planets open doors to sons, feminine planets to daughters. But the soul is beyond gender—it is eternal, only wearing this life's clothing for a little while."

In that moment, every chart became sacred. Every planet became a divine whisper. And every child, seen or unseen, was honoured as a cosmic traveller, stepping through the sky, into a waiting world.

Planets and the Five Elements: The Cosmic Tapestry of Existence

Guruji stood at the front, hands loosely folded behind his back. Before him was a painted mandala—five interlocking petals, each bearing the symbol of one of the Pancha Mahabhutas: Earth (Bhoo), Water (Jala), Fire (Agni), Air (Vaayu), and Ether (Aakaasha).

He turned slowly to the group and said:

"To understand the planets is to understand yourself. But to truly understand the planets, you must go deeper—beyond orbits and signs—to the very elements from which all creation arises."

Planet	Element (Tattva)	Core Attributes
Mars	Fire (Agni)	Energy, drive, leadership, assertiveness, business acumen
Sun	Fire (Agni)	Vitality, authority, radiance, purpose
Mercury	Earth (Bhoo)	Logic, memory, communication, practicality, organization
Saturn	Air (Vaayu)	Movement, freedom, discipline, introspection, wanderlust
Jupiter	Ether (Aakaasa)	Wisdom, higher knowledge, expansive perception, spiritual growth
Venus	Water (Jala)	Emotions, creativity, imagination, relationships, artistic sensibility
Moon	Water (Jala)	Reflective nature, emotional sensitivity, nurturing, intuition

Illustration C8: Characteristics of Planets

Guruji said, "These five elements are not just physical substances," he whispered. "They are the building blocks of both the cosmos and the soul. They exist within you, around you, and above you. And each planet governs one of these elemental forces, expressing its essence through that sacred lens."

Mars and the Sun – The Fire Element (Agni Tattva): The Flame That Moves

"Agni, the fire, is life's most dynamic force. It burns, transforms, and leads. And it is governed by Mars—the commander of energy, passion, and movement."

Guruji's eyes gleamed with intensity.

"Mars is the warrior within you—the one who pushes past hesitation, ignites willpower, and breaks inertia. In business, leadership, even survival, it is the flame of Mars that rises first."

He pointed upward.

"But Mars shares this fire with the Sun, the cosmic furnace, the ruler of vitality and dharma. While Mars is the fighter, the Sun is the sovereign—burning steadily at the centre of your being. If Mars is the spark, the Sun is the eternal flame of the soul."

He paused, letting the warmth of this truth settle in their hearts.

"Without fire, there is no initiation. Without fire, there is no direction. It is Agni that transforms potential into action."

Mercury – The Earth Element (Bhoo Tattva): The Mind That Grounds

Guruji walked slowly to the green petal representing Earth and placed his palm on it.

"Earth, or Bhoo, is form. It is stability, logic, and clarity. It is the foundation upon which ideas become structures, thoughts become words, and dreams become plans. This is the domain of Mercury, the architect of the mind."

He looked at Akanksh, "When Mercury is strong in your chart, your thoughts are organised. You speak with precision. You analyse, assess, and adapt. Like Earth, you remain firm yet fertile, capable of holding complex truths with grounded grace."

He added with a twinkle,

"But if Mercury becomes too rigid—thoughts become stubborn, and growth halts. Even Earth needs tilling to remain alive."

Saturn – The Air Element (Vaayu Tattva): The Wind That Tests and Teaches

A breeze stirred through the open window as Guruji moved to the next petal—Vaayu, air.

"Air is motion. It is discipline, distance, and detachment. It is the force that shapes without form, and the planet that governs it is Saturn—the keeper of karma."

His voice softened, reverent.

"Saturn doesn't move fast—but he moves with purpose. He creates windstorms of delay and teaches patience through passage. Like air, he cannot be held, but his presence is always felt. He whispers the lessons you don't want to hear, but must."

He turned to Vasudeva, the elder disciple known for quiet resilience.

"A person with strong Saturn may seem aloof, but inside, they carry the weight of lifetimes. And like air trapped in a flute, Saturn creates music only when embraced with structure."

Venus and the Moon – The Water Element (Jala Tattva): The Heart That Feels

Guruji said, "Water is feeling, flowing, remembering. It nourishes and dissolves. And its planets are Venus, the goddess of beauty, and the Moon, the mother of tides."

He cupped water in his hands.

"Venus governs creativity, romance, and aesthetic delight. She is the artist who paints the world in colour and song. But without emotional depth, beauty becomes shallow. This is where the Moon joins her—guiding emotion, memory, and instinct. The Moon reflects not just light, but also the hidden tides of your soul."

He turned to Roopa, whose tears sparkled at the edge of her lashes.

"If fire initiates, earth stabilises, and air tests—water is what connects. It is the river of feeling that carries us home."

Jupiter – The Ether Element (Aakaasha Tattva): The Space That Contains All

Finally, Guruji rose and pointed to the centre of the mandala, where all petals converged—a golden circle inscribed with Jupiter's symbol.

"And here," he said softly, "is Ether—Aakaasha, the silent sky. The vast, invisible canvas that holds all existence. This is governed by Jupiter, the Guru of the gods, the master of expansion."

His voice became hushed, almost like a prayer.

"Ether is not sound, but the space in which sound is heard. It is not knowledge, but the silence in which wisdom grows. Jupiter is the expansive field of insight, faith, and sacred truth. He is the sky within which all other planets move."

He gestured to the entire mandala.

"And so, Jupiter reminds you that you are more than mind, more than emotion, more than body—you are conscious space, capable of holding all things without losing yourself."

The Inner Alchemy

Guruji folded his hands and spoke with warmth:

"When you feel lost, return to the elements. If you are angry, check your fire. If restless, anchor in the earth. If numb, invite water. If heavy, let air lift you. And when all else fails—rest in ether, and simply be."

He looked at his disciples one by one.

"The planets speak through these elements—not to bind you, but to awaken you. When balanced, the five elements become the five fingers of your divine hand, shaping your life into art, your being into offering."

And with that, the wind outside paused… as if the cosmos itself had stopped to bow to the wisdom that had just descended.

Planets and Varnas: The Cosmic Order of Purpose

Akshaya, thoughtful and sincere, asked, "Guruji, we've studied the planets as rulers and deities, elements and energies. But today I read that they are also assigned **varnas**—spiritual roles, like Brahmana and Kshatriya. What does this mean?"

Guruji looked into Akshaya's eyes, smiled with understanding, and placed his palm on the centre of his chest.

"Ah, Akshaya… That question comes from the place where the **soul begins to remember.** For the planets are not only celestial forces or divine beings—they are also **archetypal roles** in the cosmic drama of life. And just as each soul carries a dharma, each planet carries a **varna**—a sacred duty, a mode of being through which it serves creation."

Planet	Varna	Key Qualities
Venus	Brahmana	Knowledge, wisdom, creativity, spiritual understanding
Jupiter	Brahmana	Higher learning, intelligence, teaching, dharma
Sun	Kshatriya	Authority, leadership, vitality, protection
Mars	Kshatriya	Bravery, strength, initiative, warrior-like energy
Mercury	Vaisya	Communication, trade, intellect, adaptability
Moon	Vaisya	Social harmony, emotions, nurturing, commerce
Saturn	Shudra	Hard work, perseverance, discipline, service

Illustration C9: Characteristics of Planets

Brahmana Planets – The Sages of Heaven (Jupiter and Venus)

In the eastern quadrant, Guruji drew the sacred symbol for **Jupiter** and **Venus**.

"These two," he said, "are the **Brahmanas**—the teachers, the spiritual torchbearers. **Jupiter**, or *Guru*, is the divine preceptor, upholding dharma, higher knowledge, and **the wisdom that guides kings and seekers alike**. Wherever he sits in the chart, he points toward the path of expansion, righteousness, and grace."

He then tapped the symbol of **Venus**.

"And **Venus**, though often seen as the planet of beauty and sensuality, is no less a Brahmana. In the Vedas, Venus is **Shukracharya**, the guru of the demons—**a master of esoteric knowledge**, a mystic who walks in the shadow, carrying light where it's least expected."

Guruji paused.

"These two remind us that **true knowledge is not just information—it is transformation.** The Brahmana planets whisper to the soul, 'You are more than this moment. Seek higher. Bow deeper.'"

Kshatriya Planets – The Warriors and Protectors (Sun and Mars)

In the southern quadrant, he drew the symbols for the **Sun** and **Mars**, and his voice became firmer—like the strike of a drum.

"The **Kshatriyas** are the warriors. They do not teach with words, but with presence. The **Sun** is the King—the ruler who embodies dharma and radiates purpose. He **leads not by fear but by example**, illuminating the way with his light."

He moved to **Mars**, and his eyes gleamed.

"**Mars** is the commander, the enforcer of divine will. He protects what is sacred. He does not hesitate—**he acts**. His courage is not reckless—it is focused, noble, and sacred. The Kshatriya planets teach us to fight our inner demons, to rise again and again, and to serve with **honour and bravery**."

He turned to **Akanksh**, who once struggled with anger.

"But remember, when misused, Mars becomes aggression, and the Sun becomes ego. Kshatriyas must be governed by wisdom, or their fire burns without light."

Vaisya Planets – The Connectors and Harmonisers (Mercury and the Moon)

Now, Guruji turned to the western quadrant, where he drew the symbols for **Mercury** and **the Moon**, his tone softening like a breeze across water.

"These are the **Vaisyas**—traders, negotiators, harmonisers. They do not rule or fight—they **connect, adapt, and circulate**. **Mercury**, the youthful prince, governs communication, intellect, business, and the weaving of thought into form. His role is to **balance**, to analyse, to interpret."

He then turned to the **Moon**, his expression tender.

"Though a Queen in the planetary cabinet, the **Moon** is a **Vaisya** in nature—**because her power lies in connection.** She flows between people, emotions, and memory. She harmonises, comforts, and reflects."

He looked at Roopa and Nita.

"The Moon doesn't fight, she doesn't command—she **soothes**. She reminds us that true strength is not always loud. Sometimes it is the **quiet presence that keeps the whole family from falling apart.**"

Shudra Planet – The Worker and Server (Saturn)

In the final quadrant, Guruji drew the glyph of **Saturn**, the servant who bears the weight of time.

"And then there is **Saturn**, the **Shudra**. The one who **works silently** while others speak. The one who endures the long night so others may wake to the dawn. He is not glamorous. He is not quick. But **he is the foundation.**"

He tapped the marble with his staff.

"Without Shudra, there is no temple. Without Saturn, there is no maturity, no karma, no evolution. His varna is humble, yes—but it is sacred. He is the one who says, *'You must walk the path. No one can do it for you.'*"

The Hidden Truth of Varnas

Guruji now stepped back, looking at the full mandala.

"These varnas are not **hierarchies of worth**. They are **frequencies of service**. Each planet, like each human being, expresses the divine through its chosen dharma."

He looked deeply into each disciple's eyes.

"You may have the fire of Mars, but the humility of Saturn. You may speak like Mercury, but think like Jupiter. The chart is not a fixed fate—it is a **divine orchestra**, and these varnas are the instruments through which **your soul plays its song**."

He closed his eyes.

"And when these planets come into balance in you… Brahmana, Kshatriya, Vaisya, and Shudra become not roles, but **states of realisation**—a full embodiment of divine potential, **from earth to ether**."

The disciples sat in awed silence, feeling not just informed—but transformed.

The planets no longer seemed distant or abstract. They had become mirrors. Roles. Archetypes. Inner teachers.

And the ancient wisdom of varna, misunderstood for centuries, had revealed itself—not as division, but as **divine design**.

Note: *The classification of planets into varnas (Brahmana, Kshatriya, Vaisya, Shudra) originates from traditional Vedic astrology and symbolises their functional attributes—not social hierarchy or human value.*

Planets and Gunas: The Symphony of Consciousness

Vidyarthi, a young seeker with bright eyes, asked, "Guruji, I understand the planets rule over signs, elements, and even varnas… but what are the **gunas**? And how do the planets reflect them?"

Guruji's face softened as he nodded. He drew three rays from the mandala's centre, forming a trinity. In each ray, he wrote one word:

- **Sattva** (purity and clarity)
- **Rajas** (activity and desire)
- **Tamas** (inertia and shadow)

Then he looked up and said with quiet gravity:

"The **gunas are not moral labels**—they are the **currents of consciousness**, the primal energies that shape all of existence. Just as every river has a current, every soul flows through a guna. And the planets—

luminous beings in the sky—carry these gunas into the very fabric of our thoughts, choices, and destinies."

Planet	Guna (Quality)	Symbolizes
Jupiter	Sattvic	Purity, wisdom, truth, spiritual growth
Moon	Sattvic	Calmness, emotional balance, nurturing nature
Sun	Sattvic	Vitality, clarity, truth, soul consciousness
Venus	Raajasik	Passion, sensuality, love, creative pursuits
Mercury	Raajasik	Intellect, communication, ambition, versatility
Saturn	Taamasik	Hardship, discipline, inertia, karmic lessons
Mars	Taamasik	Aggression, power, drive, physical action

Illustration C10: Characteristics of Planets

Sattvic Planets – Bearers of Light and Purity

(Jupiter, the Moon, and the Sun)

"Sattva," Guruji began, "is the **still flame of wisdom**. It is clarity, honesty, discernment, truth—not the truth that flatters, but the truth that liberates."

He pointed to the symbol of **Jupiter**.

"Jupiter is the great teacher—the Guru who teaches not from opinion, but from timeless understanding.

He uplifts, expands, and awakens. When you speak truth not to win, but to heal, Jupiter lives in you."

He then motioned to the **Moon**, serene in its silver beauty.

"The **Moon** in sattva is the **mind in peace**. It reflects without distortion. It nurtures without control. When you listen without judgment, when you hold space for others to feel—you're embodying the sattvic Moon."

Lastly, he turned to the **Sun**, radiant and unwavering.

"And **the Sun**, though a Kshatriya, is also sattvic. Why? Because he **shines from within**, offering life to all without attachment. His leadership is not dominance, but presence. The Sun rules the day not by demand—but by simply being himself."

Guruji smiled softly.

"Sattva is not about pleasing others. It is about being so clear, so pure in intention, that **even silence becomes guidance**."

Raajasik Planets – The Movers and Shapers

(Venus and Mercury)

Guruji's eyes now brightened as he gestured to the second ray—**rajas**.

"**Rajas** is passion, motion, desire. It's not evil—it's just **movement without stillness**. It is what drives us to create, to experience, to strive."

He pointed to **Venus**.

"**Venus** is the planet of beauty, love, and pleasure. When sattvic, Venus expresses through divine art, sacred union, and harmonious living. But in rajas, she may seek **pleasure without purpose**, becoming indulgent, possessive, even manipulative."

He then touched **Mercury's** glyph.

"**Mercury**, the messenger, is quick, clever, and adaptive. In rajas, he becomes overly analytical, always chasing stimulation—**talking more than listening, learning more than understanding**. He is the merchant who knows every price, but forgets the value."

Guruji turned to **Vidyarthi** and said:

"Rajas is not evil. It is necessary. Without rajas, no action happens. But without sattva to guide it, rajas can become **restlessness without result**—a fire with no direction."

Taamasik Planets – The Force of Resistance and Endings

(Saturn and Mars)

Now, Guruji's tone grew sombre, grounded. He walked to the third ray of the mandala: **tamas**.

"**Tamas** is heaviness, inertia, obscuration. But understand—**even the night is necessary.** Without tamas, seeds would never root. Bodies would never rest. The cycle would never renew."

He looked toward **Saturn's** glyph, etched in black.

"**Saturn** is the **guardian of tamas**. He slows. He restricts. He isolates. But in his restraint lies the **gift of endurance**. He teaches you to sit with your karma, to carry the weight without complaint. When you feel abandoned, and yet remain kind—that is Saturn working through tamas to **refine your soul**."

He turned to **Mars**, the warrior.

"Yes, **Mars** is a tamasic planet too. His force can destroy. But destruction is not always wrong—it is sometimes the only way to remove the dead wood. Mars in tamas fights with ego, not dharma. He reacts, not responds."

Guruji's eyes met those of each disciple.

"Tamas becomes dangerous only when misunderstood. **Handled with awareness, it becomes the doorway to stillness, to grounding, to death of the false self.**"

The Dance of the Three

He stepped back from the mandala and drew a spiral that connected all three rays.

"All three gunas exist in everyone. Even the planets themselves are not fixed—they **express differently based on context**. Saturn, when purified, becomes the servant of truth. Venus, when elevated, becomes the consort of divine art. The Sun, when egoic, can even slip from sattva to rajas."

He paused, letting the silence speak.

"The gunas are not enemies. They are **threads of a single loom**. Sattva brings light. Rajas brings motion. Tamas brings rest. Together, they weave the **fabric of life.** Your work is not to escape them, but to **master them.**"

He placed his hand over his heart.

"When sattva is your guide, rajas your fuel, and tamas your ground—you live as a complete being. You act without ego, speak without harm, and rest without fear."

The True Sadhana

As the disciples sat in profound stillness, Guruji said:

"Vidyarthi, when you study the gunas in a chart, don't just see them as attributes of planets. **See them in your own breath**. Are you acting from clarity, or from need? Are you silent from wisdom, or from numbness? Every moment, you are under the influence of a guna. And in every moment, you have the chance to choose—**not what you feel, but how you respond.**"

And as the wind outside whispered through the trees, something timeless stirred within the hearts of all who listened.

For in that moment, the planets stopped being symbols…
and became mirrors.

Coffee Break Under the Banyan Tree — Apeksha's Reflection in Kanchipuram

The midday sun in **Kanchipuram** was mellow, softened by the dappled shade of an ancient **banyan tree** whose roots had whispered stories into the soil for centuries. It stood just beyond the temple corridor, a living canopy with arms that cradled not only birds and breezes—but seekers.

A small group of disciples had gathered beneath it for what began as a simple **coffee break**, but which, in true Guruji fashion, was turning into something far more sacred.

Vasudeva leaned against one of the aerial roots, a steaming steel tumbler in his hand, as he spoke thoughtfully to **Vidyarthi**, who was scribbling notes even as he sipped. **Aastha** and **Abhirami** sat cross-legged nearby on a red cotton mat, passing around a tin of biscuits. **Kiran** and **Sam** were locked in playful debate, while **Alice**, **Sofia**, **Bhavya**, and **Aarna** listened with amused smiles, the wind tugging gently at their scarves.

And watching them all—**Apeksha** sat quietly to the side, her back resting against the broad trunk of the banyan. From her vantage point, it felt as though **each person was a planet**, and the banyan their shared solar system.

She closed her eyes for a moment… and in that stillness, a story began to unfold—not from memory, but from intuition.

Vasudeva – The Sun Resting in the Temple of Thought

Apeksha saw **Vasudeva** as the **Sun**—radiant, authoritative, deeply respected. His questions often pierced like sunrays, illuminating areas others hadn't yet dared to explore.

Today, his words about *dharma* and *selfless service* echoed like temple bells. He was the **King of the planetary cabinet**, yet there was humility in the way he waited for everyone to speak.

"Vasudeva," she thought, "is like the Sun seated in a temple—quietly watching, silently guiding, holding the space with warmth."

Vidyarthi – The Moon by the Waters of Reflection

Vidyarthi, ever contemplative, reminded her of the **Moon**—fluid, emotional, intelligent. He never interrupted but absorbed everything, letting wisdom settle in him like moonlight on still water.

When he asked softly, *"But isn't even rajas necessary to cross over to sattva?"*, everyone paused. It was the kind of question that didn't seek an answer, but evoked one from within.

"He's the Moon by the riverbank," Apeksha smiled, "gathering truth drop by drop."

Aastha – Mars in the Arena of Spirit

Aastha was Mars—not in anger, but in **courage**. She spoke with clarity and stood with certainty. Even as she poured the filter coffee, her gestures carried strength and purpose.

When **Kiran** laughed, teasing her for being "too serious," she just raised an eyebrow and said, *"Discipline is also devotion."*

"She is Mars in the arena of the spirit," Apeksha mused, "graceful, fierce, unwavering."

Abhirami – Venus in the Chamber of Quiet Beauty

Abhirami, sitting beside Aastha, was a quiet Venus. There was gentleness in her voice, elegance in the way she passed the biscuits, and poetry in the way she described the jasmine blooming by the temple wall.

She didn't speak often, but when she did, hearts leaned in.

"Venus," Apeksha thought, "in her truest home—the bedroom of the soul, where beauty is intimacy, and intimacy is reverence."

Kiran – Mercury in the Stadium of Thought

Kiran, with his quips and questions, was **Mercury** at full play—quick-witted, analytical, sparring with ideas like a child dancing between sunbeams. He teased **Sam**, challenged **Vidyarthi**, and even poked light fun at **Vasudeva**—with equal parts charm and respect.

"He is Mercury in his stadium," Apeksha smiled, "turning intellect into a game, and the game into insight."

Sam – Saturn in the Alley of Real Talk

Sam had the dry humour of **Saturn**, often pointing out what others politely ignored. When someone spilled the coffee, he muttered, *"Spilled karma, incoming lessons,"* and everyone laughed—but also thought.

He wasn't afraid to talk about suffering, nor to sit with silence. There was something steady, even sacred, in his raw honesty.

"Sam is Saturn dwelling in the alleys of experience," Apeksha realised. "Rough-edged but truthful."

Alice and Sofia – The Twin Breezes of Rajas and Sattva

Alice and **Sofia** were like twin aspects of the **air element**—light, curious, floating between **sattva** and **rajas**. They asked questions about **Gunatraya**, debated the difference between emotional reaction and intuitive action, and still found time to marvel at the silk sarees drying on nearby steps.

They were Mercury and Moon, perhaps—**reflective and radiant**, expressive and open.

"They bring balance," Apeksha thought, "as if the wind in them stirs others into movement."

Bhavya – Jupiter with a Smile Full of Stars

Bhavya had the glow of **Jupiter**—not loud, but unmistakably luminous. She had a way of tying threads together, grounding ideas, and giving others a sense of trust. When she spoke of **Guruji's teaching on planetary gunas**, it wasn't an explanation—it was an offering.

"She's Jupiter dwelling in a house full of treasures," Apeksha noted. "Only her treasure is kindness, and it spills into every conversation."

Aarna – Ether Holding All Things

And then there was **Aarna**, the quietest of them all, watching everything like the **sky watches the stars**. She said little but seemed to understand much—like ether, like space, **the container of all the rest**.

"She is Jupiter's aakaasha," Apeksha thought, "not in speech, but in silence."

And Apeksha – The Seer Between Worlds

And what of **Apeksha** herself?

She didn't know. Perhaps she was a little of everyone. Perhaps she was the tree—the witness. Or perhaps she was **the breeze beneath the banyan**, listening, feeling, reflecting, recording.

She took a sip of her coffee and let the moment stretch—**a sip from a stainless steel tumbler, a taste of cosmic tea**, brewed from planets, elements, varnas, and gunas… shared among friends beneath a tree older than memory.

In that simple break, under a banyan in Kanchipuram, something more than coffee had been poured.

A gathering of planets had come together—not to debate, not to shine—but to be.

And for Apeksha, it was a moment she would carry like a constellation in her heart.

CHAPTER II

The Mystical Attributes II

"To know the stars is not to escape destiny, but to understand its language—so we may walk our path not in fear, but with reverence and purpose." — Shree Shambav

Planetary Abodes: The Homes of the Divine Within

Vidyarthi, thoughtful and contemplative, turned to Guruji and asked, "Guruji, we've spoken of the planets as rulers, as warriors, as deities, and as teachers… but where do they rest? Where do they *live*?"

Guruji smiled—not the smile of someone amused, but of someone quietly moved.

"Ah," he said, "a soul only asks about a being's home when it's ready to see them **as real**."

He rose and walked toward the sacred mandala on the floor, which now had seven doors drawn around a central flame—each doorway representing an abode, a world, a space of resonance.

Planet	Dwelling Place	Symbolism
Sun	Temple	Purity, divinity, spirituality, higher purpose
Moon	Near water	Emotions, intuition, fluidity, nurturing energy
Mercury	Stadium	Intellect, communication, adaptability, mental agility
Jupiter	Treasure-filled home	Wisdom, prosperity, abundance, spiritual wealth
Venus	Bedroom	Love, beauty, comfort, sensuality, personal relationships
Saturn	Unclean places	Hardship, discipline, endurance, karmic challenges

Illustration C11: Characteristics of Planets

"Let me show you," he said. "The abodes of the planets are not mere symbols. They are reflections of where each energy feels *most at home*—in the outer world, yes, but more importantly, in your inner landscape. To know their homes is to know their heart."

The Sun – Dweller of Temples

Guruji stood before the **first doorway**, shaped like a **temple spire**, rising skyward.

"The **Sun** dwells in temples," he said. "Not for luxury or comfort—but for **purpose, purity, and presence.** A temple is where you go to remember who you are. It is a space of light, silence, and unwavering truth."

He turned to **Vasudeva**, who once sought validation through status.

"The Sun teaches that real power doesn't come from pride—it comes from **alignment with dharma**. Like the Sun resting in a sanctum, you too must rest in your truth. When the Sun is at home in you, you radiate with integrity—not to impress, but to **inspire**."

The Moon – At Home by Water

He moved to the **next doorway**, framed by flowing waves and soft reflections.

"The **Moon** lives by the water," he whispered. "A riverbank, a quiet lake, the ocean under moonlight—these are her abodes. She needs space to feel, to reflect, to flow."

Guruji looked at **Roopa**, who often hid her feelings behind a calm face.

"When the Moon is at home in you, **tears become sacred**, and emotions are not weakness—they are the currents that connect you to the soul. Like water, the Moon teaches you to be gentle yet deep, changing yet timeless."

Mercury – The Stadium Dweller

At the third doorway, there was **laughter, motion, noise, and intellect**—the energy of a **stadium or marketplace**.

"**Mercury** lives in places full of **dialogue, trade, play, and motion**," Guruji said. "A stadium, a classroom, a debate hall—these are his temples. He is the mind that loves the **game of learning**, the **dance of words**, the art of adapting."

He smiled at **Akanksh**, who had once been overwhelmed by overthinking.

"When Mercury is at home in you, your mind is not scattered—it is **alive**, responsive, and joyful. It learns by doing, understands by sharing. It teaches you that communication is not just noise—it is **connection**."

Jupiter – Dweller of Treasure-Filled Homes

The next doorway shimmered with **books, scrolls, altars, and abundance**—a home filled not with gold, but with **knowledge**.

"**Jupiter** resides in a home full of **treasures**—not of material wealth alone, but of **wisdom, values, family, and faith.** He governs the sanctity of the home where learning is respected and elders are honoured."

Guruji touched his heart and said,

"When Jupiter is at home in you, you walk with grace. You speak with purpose. You believe not just in yourself, but in the **goodness of life**. This abode is one of inner fullness—a wealth that can never be stolen."

Venus – Queen of the Bedroom

He turned to a doorway draped with silk, scented with roses, glowing softly with candlelight.

"**Venus** makes her home in the **bedroom**," he said, "because it is the space of **intimacy, pleasure, sensuality, and beauty.** But not just carnal pleasure—**the pleasure of feeling alive**, of being seen, touched, and loved."

He looked at **Aastha**, whose heart longed for connection but feared vulnerability.

"When Venus is at home in you, your life becomes a **work of art**. You learn that beauty is not vanity—it is an offering. That love is not weakness—it is the **path of union**."

Saturn – Resident of the Unclean and Forgotten

At the final doorway, a broken gate, worn and dusty, led into a **dark alley** filled with tools, sweat, and silence.

"And **Saturn**," he said, "makes his abode in the **unclean, the forgotten, the hard places**—where no one else wants to live."

He looked at the disciples with gravity.

"Why? Because Saturn is the **servant of truth**. He finds divinity in discipline, in effort, in **rising through the mud**. When Saturn is at home in you, you no longer avoid suffering—you transmute it. You sweep the temple floor not with shame, but with honour."

He turned to **Padma**, who had endured many trials with quiet grace.

"Saturn shows you that there is **dignity in the dark**, and that light is most meaningful when it has passed through shadow."

The Inner Homes

Guruji stood at the centre of the seven doorways and spoke with a quiet authority that filled the room:

"Each planet has its place. And within you, each of these places exists. You are the temple. You are the ocean. You are the stadium, the library, the bedroom, the alleyway."

He placed a hand over his chest.

"When you understand where these planets dwell—not just out there, but **within you**—you begin to see life not as a series of problems, but as a **sacred architecture.** Every room in your inner house has a purpose. Every planet is a guest—**and your soul is the host.**"

The silence that followed was not empty.

It was a homecoming.

The Sapta Dhaatus: The Sacred Alchemy of Body and Cosmos

Padma, with folded hands, asked the question: "Guruji, we've studied the grahas, the varnas, the elements, the gunas… but what of this body that houses them all? How is the human form related to the planets?"

Guruji closed his eyes for a moment, as if listening to a memory deeper than thought. Then he opened them slowly and spoke:

"Ah, … The body is not just a shell. It is a **temple made of stars**, built with care, intelligence, and purpose. Just as the universe is composed of the five elements, the **human form is composed of seven sacred building blocks**—the *Sapta Dhaatus*. And each is ruled by a planet."

Dhaatu (Element)	Governing Planet	Symbolism
Bones	Sun	Strength, structure, foundation of the body
Blood	Moon	Fluids, emotions, circulation, nurturing energy
Marrow	Mars	Vitality, energy, life force
Skin	Mercury	Communication, sensitivity, interaction with the world
Fat	Jupiter	Nourishment, insulation, growth and expansion
Semen/ Reproductive Fluid	Venus	Fertility, creativity, procreation
Muscles	Saturn	Endurance, hard work, movement and effort

Illustration C12: Characteristics of Planets

1. Bones – Ruled by the Sun (Surya)

"The **bones**," Guruji began, placing his hand firmly on his spine, "are governed by **Surya**, the Sun—the radiant king who gives structure to the body as he gives dharma to the world. Without bones, there is no form; without dharma, there is no direction."

He turned to **Vasudeva**, whose quiet authority often held the group together.

"When the Sun is strong in you, your bones stand tall—so too does your sense of purpose. But when afflicted, it is as if the **temple pillars begin to crack**, and one forgets who they are."

2. Blood – Ruled by the Moon (Chandra)

"The **Moon rules the blood**, the sacred river within, flowing with memory, emotion, and life force," he continued, touching his wrist where the pulse danced.

He looked to **Padma**, known for her empathy and deep emotional intelligence.

"Just as the Moon pulls the ocean tides, she stirs the **inner ocean** of our emotions. When she is balanced, your blood sings with vitality and peace. But when she is troubled… emotions surge, blood may weaken, and the inner tides become stormy."

3. Marrow – Ruled by Mars (Mangala)

"Deep within the bones lies the **marrow**, governed by **Mars**, the warrior of life," Guruji said with a spark in his eyes. "Marrow produces blood cells, carries immunity, and fuels vitality. It is the silent fire within."

He pointed toward **Akshaya**, whose energy was focused, powerful, and raw.

"Mars is not just aggression—it is the **drive to live**. A strong Mars gives you vitality; a weak Mars may leave your body **like a fortress without soldiers**—prone to infection, fatigue, and depletion."

4. Skin – Ruled by Mercury (Budha)

Guruji softly brushed his hand along his forearm.

"The **skin**, our boundary with the world, is ruled by **Mercury**. Sensitive, responsive, intelligent—it is the interface between the self and the other. It absorbs, reflects, and communicates—just like Budha."

He turned to **Espen**, the calm, thoughtful listener.

"When Mercury is clear, your skin is healthy, your communication is smooth. But if Mercury is clouded—**the body becomes reactive**, and words, like skin, may become inflamed."

5. Fat – Ruled by Jupiter (Guru)

"**Fat**, or *medas*, is often misunderstood," Guruji said, lifting his cup of warm milk. "But in Ayurveda, fat is nourishment—it protects, insulates, supports fertility. It is governed by **Jupiter**, the giver of abundance."

He looked at **Bhavya**, whose nurturing presence seemed to feed everyone's spirit.

"A well-aspected Jupiter blesses you with **gentle strength**. But excess, or deficiency, reveals a Jupiter out of balance—**too much indulgence, or too little nourishment**—both are forms of disconnection from wisdom."

6. Semen (Reproductive Essence) – Ruled by Venus (Shukra)

Guruji's voice softened as he addressed the most sacred of dhaatus.

"The **reproductive essence**, the seed of life itself, is ruled by **Venus**. In men, it is semen; in women, it is an ovum. But beyond biology, it is **creativity, pleasure, intimacy, the sacred act of giving life—physical or spiritual**."

He gazed at **Apeksha**, the silent dreamer who painted the world with words.

"When Venus is exalted, this essence becomes **inspiration**. When disturbed, it becomes either indulgence or repression. The balance of Venus is not restraint—it is **reverence**."

7. Muscles – Ruled by Saturn (Shani)

Finally, Guruji tapped his own bicep lightly and said:

"The **muscles**—the flesh that labours—are ruled by **Saturn**, the slow, enduring servant of karma. Muscles move the body not with speed, but **through habit, through repetition, through discipline.**"

He turned to **Sujitha**, who never complained, even when the work was difficult.

"A strong Saturn builds not just strength, but **resilience**. A weak Saturn may result in fatigue, fragility, or fear of endurance. But when you serve with humility, Saturn becomes your greatest ally."

The Hidden Harmony

Guruji sat back on his asana and looked at his disciples with infinite compassion.

"The seven dhaatus are not just tissues. They are **echoes of planets within the body**. The health of each planet determines the **quality of the substance**, the flow of energy, the nature of your response to the world."

He paused.

"If one dhaatu is weak, the body suffers. If one planet is in pain, the soul cries through the body. This is why Vedic astrology is not just a tool of prediction—it is a map for healing. Your chart is not a sentence—it is a **prescription.**"

And as the bells from the nearby temple rang out in soft waves, the truth became clear:

They were not separate from the stars. The stars had simply taken form within them.

Planets and Time Periods: The Celestial Rhythm of Becoming

It was a luminous afternoon in Kanchipuram, and the Buddha Hall had quieted after a morning of intense teachings. The scent of sandalwood drifted lazily through the air.

Aarna, thoughtful and introspective asked, "Guruji, we often speak of the planets in our charts, their traits and alignments. But how do they shape *time* itself? Do they govern the rhythm of our days and years?"

Guruji looked up at her with a gaze that held lifetimes.

Guruji said, "You've asked a question that touches not just the stars, but the pulse of time itself. Time is not linear—it is **cyclical**, **sacred**, and **deeply personal**. Each planet governs a **specific heartbeat of time**, and when you learn to listen… you realise that the cosmos is not above you. It is moving *through* you."

He gestured to the nearby stone path that spiralled outward from a lotus carving in the earth.

"Come, let me tell you a story. A story of how **Time itself walks with the planets.**"

The Sun – Guardian of the Ayana (Half-Year Cycle)

Guruji began with the **Sun**, the unwavering centre.

"The **Sun**, sovereign and constant, governs the **Ayana**—a six-month cycle of purpose. It does not race like the Moon or spark like Mars. It moves with stately grace, marking two great arcs: **Uttarayana**, when it moves north, and **Dakshinayana**, when it moves south."

Planet	Time Period Governed	Symbolic Significance
Sun	Ayana (Half-Year Cycle)	Represents vitality, consistency, and the solar journey
Moon	Minutes	Reflects rapid changes, emotions, and fluid mental states
Mars	Weeks	Symbolizes energy, initiative, and short-term actions
Mercury	Ritus (Seasons)	Denotes adaptation, transitions, and intellectual flexibility
Jupiter	Months	Represents growth, wisdom, and expansive cycles
Venus	Fortnights (15-day periods)	Symbolizes harmony, beauty, and balanced rhythms
Saturn	Year	Denotes endurance, karma, long-term discipline, and life structure

Illustration C13A: Characteristics of Planets

He pointed to the sky.

"When the Sun moves north—from **Capricorn to Gemini**—it brings light, action, aspiration. This is *Uttarayana*, the ascent of consciousness. And when it descends—from **Cancer to Sagittarius**—*Dakshinayana*—it invites inwardness, reflection, humility."

He turned to Aarna.

"The Sun teaches us: true purpose is not rushed. It is a half-year dance of **becoming and unbecoming**, blooming and resting, breathing in and breathing out."

Movement	Zodiac Range	Description
Uttarayana	Capricorn (Makara) → Gemini (Mithuna)	The Sun's northward journey; associated with spiritual progress and light
Dakshinayana	Cancer (Karka) → Sagittarius (Dhanu)	The Sun's southward journey; associated with introspection and karmic work

Illustration C13B: Characteristics of Planets

The Moon – Ruler of Minutes, Mistress of Emotion

"The **Moon**, on the other hand," Guruji said, tracing a circle in the air, "is the breath of time itself. She rules **minutes**, fleeting and sacred."

He paused.

"Why minutes? Because she governs **change**—of mood, of tides, of thoughts. Her phases are the soul's mirror. You may be joyful one moment, sorrowful the next. This is not weakness. This is the **Moon marking time in feelings.**"

He looked at Padma, whose empathy often overwhelmed her.

"When the Moon governs you, learn to honour your minutes—not to control them, but to feel them fully.

She teaches that in a single moment, your entire sky can shift."

Mars – The Pulse of Weeks

Guruji after a pause said, "Mars, the warrior, governs weeks—a span of time where momentum builds and actions matter. Weeks are not as fleeting as minutes, but not as enduring as months. They are the time it takes to fight a battle, to start a habit, to test strength."

He smiled at Akshaya, whose drive was relentless.

"When Mars is strong, a week can reshape your life. But if misused, weeks become **wounds**. Mars reminds us: *what you do this week echoes for months to come.*"

Mercury – Lord of Ritus (Seasons)

He gestured to the breeze that had just shifted.

"Ah, **Mercury**, the playful, clever messenger, rules the **Ritus**—the six seasons of the Indian calendar. Each ritu lasts about **two months**, embodying the cycle of **transformation and adaptation**."

He recited the names slowly, reverently:

- **Vasanta (Spring)** – Joy and rebirth
- **Greeshma (Summer)** – Intensity and assertion

- **Varsha (Monsoon)** – Cleansing and emotion
- **Sharad (Autumn)** – Balance and beauty
- **Hemanta (Pre-Winter)** – Gathering and reflection
- **Shishira (Winter)** – Rest and stillness

"Just like Mercury," he said, "ritual requires you to adjust, to shift rhythm and language. You can't wear monsoon shoes in summer. And you can't use summer fire in winter introspection."

Ritu (Season)	English Name	Description
Vasanta	Spring	Season of renewal, blooming, and freshness
Greeshma	Summer	Season of heat, dryness, and intensity
Varsha	Rainy Season	Season of rainfall, nourishment, and fertility
Hemanta	Dewy Season	Cool and misty period post-monsoon
Seeta	Winter	Cold season, often marked by stillness
Sisira	Autumn/Fall	Season of shedding, balance, and preparation

Illustration C13C: Characteristics of Planets

He winked.

"Mercury teaches us that **true intelligence is seasonal.**"

Jupiter – Guardian of the Months

"**Jupiter**, the Guru, rules **months**—the time it takes for learning to unfold, for **growth to take root.** It is in months that seeds sprout, wisdom matures, and ideas deepen."

He looked at **Vidyarthi**, whose hunger for knowledge was insatiable.

"When Jupiter governs your time, don't rush. One month can teach more than a year, if your mind is **open and willing.** Jupiter teaches that knowledge grows **slowly but surely**—like a tree that does not bloom until its roots are strong."

Venus – Ruler of Fortnights (Pakshas)

He now drew a crescent moon, waxing and waning.

"**Venus** rules the **Paksha**—the **fortnight**, from New Moon to Full, from Full to New. It is a cycle of **balance, beauty, and recalibration**. Fifteen days to love, to heal, to realign."

He turned to Abhirami, the artist whose paintings seemed to breathe.

"Venus teaches you to *feel deeply but act rhythmically.* A paksha is the time between two longings, between creation and rest. In these two-week rhythms, you learn to harmonise your inner world with the outer."

Saturn – The Keeper of the Year

Finally, Guruji picked up a dried leaf and placed it in his palm.

"And then comes **Saturn**—the slow, wise teacher who governs the **year**. A year is the time required for *karma to speak clearly*, for **discipline to show its fruits**."

He looked at Sujitha, whose quiet endurance had carried her through many storms.

"A Saturn year does not shout. It walks slowly beside you, testing your faith, strengthening your spine. You may not see its gift until the end—but when it comes, it is permanent."

Time as a Temple

Guruji now rose fully and stretched his arms out to the sky.

"Do you see, my children? Time is not a ticking clock. It is a temple, and each planet is its priest—marking sacred rites of passage, from breath to year, from moment to transformation."

He turned back to Aarna, now teary-eyed.

"To live astrologically is not to be ruled by time. It is to be in rhythm with it. When you know what time it is cosmically, you stop rushing… and start aligning."

The disciples bowed their heads, not to the sky, but to the silence between seconds.

Because in that pause, they felt it:

Time was not passing.

Time was whispering.

And they had just remembered how to listen.

Planets and Tastes: The Celestial Flavours of Life

It was just before the midday meal at the **Kanchipuram ashram**, and the scent of cumin and ghee wafted through the open windows of the kitchen. The disciples had just returned from their session beneath the ancient banyan tree, minds steeped in planetary wisdom, hearts gently stretched with awe.

Vasudeva, ever thoughtful, walked beside **Guruji** as they approached the dining hall. The clinking of vessels, the hiss of steam, and the melodic rhythm of ladles stirring sabzi filled the air.

As they sat on the veranda facing the garden, Vasudeva asked quietly:

"Guruji, if the planets influence time, body, and mind… do they also influence our **tastes**—our food, our cravings, even our eating habits?"

Guruji smiled, his gaze softening like sugar melting into warm milk.

"Ah, Vasudeva," he said, "a wise question indeed. Just as each planet sings its song into your bones and breath, it also whispers into your **tongue**—through the **rasas**, the six fundamental tastes. Every flavour you crave, every dish you avoid, every spice that stirs something ancient in your soul—it is **not random.** It is **cosmic memory unfolding on your plate.**"

Planet	Taste	Examples	Symbolism
Sun	Pungent	Onions, ginger, pepper	Vitality, stimulation, intensity
Moon	Salty	Sea salt, rock salt	Emotional depth, fluidity
Mars	Bitter	Bitter gourd (karela), dandelion root, neem, rhubarb	Purification, discipline, sharp energy
Mercury	Mixed/Balanced	Harmonious blends of multiple tastes	Adaptability, communication, balance
Jupiter	Sweet	Sugar, dates, milk-based sweets	Growth, nourishment, generosity
Venus	Sour	Lemon, tamarind, fermented foods	Desire, attraction, emotional stimulation
Saturn	Astringent	Plantain, pomegranate, unripe banana, lentils	Restraint, discipline, cleansing

Illustration C14: Characteristics of Planets

The Sun – Pungent Taste: The Fire That Awakens

Guruji began with the **Sun**, as always.

"The **Sun**, the sovereign of the solar system, governs the **pungent taste**—strong, sharp, stimulating. Onions, black pepper, ginger—these are foods that ignite the fire, **activate digestion**, and awaken the senses."

He pointed to a slice of ginger on his plate.

"This is Surya's food. It purifies. It challenges. It *demands presence.* Just like the Sun, it brings heat, clarity, and purpose. But too much, and it can **burn**—just like unchecked ego or pride."

He glanced at **Vasudeva,** who often led others with gentle dignity.

"When the Sun rules your second house, you may crave pungent food—but you must use it as **fuel for focus**, not indulgence."

The Moon – Salty Taste: The Ocean Within

Next, he touched a bowl of rock salt on the banana leaf.

"The **Moon** rules **salty flavours**, Vasudeva. Think of the oceans, the tears, the blood that carries salt—**these are the Moon's expressions.** Salt is grounding. It preserves. It enhances."

He looked at **Padma**, who was nearby, preparing water with a pinch of Himalayan salt.

"But too much salt in a Moon period—especially during emotional storms—can **aggravate the waters** within. The Moon brings emotional tides, and salt strengthens them. Learn when to taste, and when to *fast.* The Moon teaches us that even flavour needs stillness."

Mars – Bitter Taste: The Warrior's Elixir

Guruji then took a small piece of **karela (bitter gourd)** from his thali and raised it with reverence.

"**Mars** rules the **bitter taste**, which is perhaps the most **misunderstood**. Neem, dandelion, karela… These are not foods of pleasure, but of **purification.** They cleanse the liver, reduce excess, cut through heat."

He turned to **Akshaya**, who often thrived on discipline and challenge.

"Bitter foods teach what Mars teaches: **not all good things are sweet.** Sometimes what heals you most… is what tastes harsh. The warrior in you must learn to **digest bitterness with grace.**"

Mercury – Mixed Tastes: The Alchemy of Balance

Pointing to a spoonful of **avial**, a South Indian dish that mixed flavours with harmony, Guruji continued:

"**Mercury**, the master of adaptability, rules **mixed tastes**—a little sweet, a little tangy, a hint of spice. This is the food of the **intellect**, the communicator. It reflects a mind that can **blend and adapt**, like spices dancing together in one dish."

He smiled at **Espen**, who was always experimenting with new combinations.

"A Mercury-dominant person might crave novelty in food—flavours that surprise, combinations that challenge. But the lesson is to find *harmony*, not confusion. Let your plate reflect your **mental state**."

Jupiter – Sweet Taste: The Nourishment of Trust

Guruji now pointed to a date and a spoonful of rice with jaggery.

"**Jupiter**, the guru, rules the **sweet taste**—nourishing, calming, expansive. This is the food of **contentment**, of **childhood**, of **trust.**"

He turned to **Bhavya**, whose very presence seemed to soothe those around her.

"When Jupiter governs your second house, you may gravitate to sweets—not out of craving, but out of a soul-memory of **being held by life.** But beware—too much sugar, and expansion turns into **excess**, comfort into **complacency.** Jupiter teaches balance in generosity."

Venus – Sour Taste: The Tang of Desire

Guruji now placed a slice of lemon on his tongue, his expression thoughtful.

"**Venus** governs the **sour taste**—tamarind, lemon, fermented foods. Sour flavours stir the senses, **awaken**

the appetite, and ignite **longing**. This is the taste of **pleasure and passion.**"

He looked at **Abhirami**, whose art captured longing without words.

"Venusian food is not just about eating—it's about **feeling**, tasting beauty, *desiring deeply*. But too much sourness during Venus periods can lead to emotional acidity—**longing without fulfilment**. Venus teaches: taste your desires, but do not drown in them."

Saturn – Astringent Taste: The Humble Cleanser

Finally, Guruji held up a piece of **plantain** and a slice of **pomegranate**.

"And then there is **Saturn**—ruler of the **astringent taste**. It is the driest, the most contracting. Think of raw banana, green tea, and pomegranate. These are not festive foods. They are **ritual foods**—cleansing, binding, stabilising."

He nodded toward **Sujitha**, whose strength lay in quiet perseverance.

"Saturn's foods remind us that life is not always sweet or spicy. Sometimes it is plain. Restrained. Bare. But in that barrenness lies **truth**, **discipline**, and **cleansing.** Astringent taste is the food of **monastics and seekers.** It is where indulgence ends, and **clarity begins.**"

The Tongue as a Compass, the Plate as a Chart

Guruji leaned back, eyes glimmering.

"You see, Vasudeva, your cravings are not flaws—they are **messages.** The tongue is the **astrologer of the body**. The food you reach for is often the flavour your soul is trying to process."

He added with a soft chuckle:

"And during certain planetary periods—like Jupiter dasa or Moon antardasa—certain tastes **amplify or hinder healing**. A salt-heavy diet during a disturbed Moon phase may worsen your blood pressure or emotions. Too much sweetness during Jupiter's transit may cause **expansion where contraction is needed.**"

Eating as Offering, Taste as Teaching

The lunch bell rang in the distance, and the disciples slowly began walking toward the dining hall.

Guruji whispered one final teaching:

"Eat not to fill, but to **feel**. Taste is not just physical—it is planetary, spiritual, karmic. And when you understand the rasa of your food, you understand the **rasa of your life.**"

As Vasudeva joined the others, a quiet smile played on his lips.

His hunger was not just for food anymore—but for the understanding that every bite was a **cosmic echo**…a sacred flavour from the stars.

CHAPTER III

The Mystical Attributes III

"The planets do not command us; they compose us—each one a brushstroke in the masterpiece of our becoming." — Shree Shambav.

Planetary Strengths: The Secret Pulse Behind the Stars

It was just after lunch in the **Buddha Hall**. The air was thick with the earthy scent of sandalwood and the mellow calm that follows a satisfying meal. Outside, the temple bells chimed faintly, synchronising with the rhythmic sighs of banyan leaves rustling under the weight of early summer.

The intensity of the morning teachings had mellowed into a meditative stillness, where every word felt more like a breath than a lecture.

And then Guruji began again, his voice warm as the sunlight that filtered through the carved stone lattice.

"Now that the body has been nourished, let us speak of strength—not of the body, but of the planets. For each graha has its moment, its direction, its moon phase, its hour. And when you align your life with the **strength of the planets**, you stop fighting fate… and start flowing with it."

Digbala: The Directional Pulse of the Cosmos

Guruji rose and walked slowly to the centre of the Hall, where a **mandala of directions** had been drawn earlier in the morning session. He took a stick of sandalwood chalk and began drawing four luminous arrows—East, South, West, North.

Planet	Direction of Strength	Associated House	Notes
Mercury	East	1st House (Lagna/Ascendant)	Gains strength at the beginning of life paths
Jupiter	East	1st House (Lagna/Ascendant)	Symbolizes wisdom, clarity, and growth
Sun	South	10th House (Meridian)	Represents power, authority, and ambition
Mars	South	10th House (Meridian)	Indicates action, courage, and discipline
Moon	North	4th House (Nadir)	Reflects emotions, inner life, and comfort
Venus	North	4th House (Nadir)	Relates to beauty, love, and harmony
Saturn	West	7th House (Descendant)	Governs discipline, endurance, and maturity

Illustration C15A: Characteristics of Planets

"Just as the sun rises in the east and sets in the west, so too do the planets have their favoured stages, their most powerful orientations. This is called **Digbala**, the strength of direction."

East – The Dawn of Wisdom

"**Mercury and Jupiter** rise in the **East**," he said, looking toward Vidyarthi.

"The East is the Lagna—where life begins. It's where knowledge awakens, where curiosity breathes. When these planets are placed here, they lend **clarity, insight, and grace at the start of every endeavour.**"

South – The Domain of Karma

He turned to Akshaya.

"**Mars and the Sun** shine in the **South**, the 10th house—**the house of karma**. This is where purpose, willpower, and responsibility unfold. It is the battlefield of dharma, the zenith of the soul's journey."

North – The Cave of the Heart

Then to Padma, he said:

"**Venus and the Moon** rest in the **North**, the 4th house. This is the **womb of memory**, of emotion, of home. When these planets are strong here, **nurturing becomes a divine act**."

West – The Discipline of Time

Finally, turning to Sujitha:

"**Saturn rules the West**, the 7th house, the setting Sun. He gains strength in endings, in restraint, in the quiet duty of relationship and legacy. To have Saturn strong here is to walk the world with **gravity and grace.**"

Time and Strength – When Planets Speak Loudest

Guruji sat again, his voice steady and low.

"But direction is not all. **Time is a gatekeeper.** Each graha has its hour, its mood, its pulse."

Planet	Time of Strength	Notes
Moon	Night	Reflects inner emotions, intuition, and calmness
Mars	Night	Gains assertiveness and courage during the night
Saturn	Night	Strengthens endurance, discipline, and reflection
Sun	Day	Radiates authority, leadership, and clarity
Jupiter	Day	Enhances wisdom, growth, and optimism
Venus	Day	Brings beauty, love, and harmony to the forefront
Mercury	Day & Night (Always)	Constantly strong—adaptable, intelligent, neutral

Illustration C15B: Characteristics of Planets

Day Planets – Sun, Jupiter, Venus

"These are the planets of light. They govern action, learning, and love. They shine from dawn to dusk, guiding the outward journey."

Night Planets – Moon, Mars, Saturn

"These are the planets of inner work, dreams, protection, and surrender. They speak not with volume—but with vision. They whisper in the night what the day cannot teach."

Mercury – The Constant Messenger

"Mercury is neither of the night nor the day. He is **everywhere**—the witness, the scribe, the bridge. His strength is in **fluidity.**"

Lunar and Solar Strengths – The Breath of the Sky

As the wind entered through the temple windows, Guruji continued:

Waxing Moon – Strength of the Benefics

"When the Moon waxes, **Jupiter and Venus** glow with it. This is a time for growth, creation, and harmony."

Waning Moon – Strength of the Malefics

"When the Moon wanes, **Mars, Saturn, Rahu, and Ketu** gather strength. This is a time of facing fears, refining purpose, and breaking illusions."

Sun's Course:

- **Uttarayana** (Capricorn to Gemini): Benefics shine.
- **Dakshinayana** (Cancer to Sagittarius): Malefics rise.

Condition	Planets Gaining Strength	Notes
Krishna Paksha (Waning Moon)	Natural Malefics (Mars, Saturn, Rahu, Ketu)	Their intense, transformative energies are amplified
Shukla Paksha (Waxing Moon)	Natural Benefics (Jupiter, Venus)	Favourable, nurturing energies are enhanced
Dakshina Ayana (Sun: Cancer → Sagittarius)	Natural Malefics	Energies of discipline, challenge, and inner work are strengthened
Uttara Ayana (Sun: Capricorn → Gemini)	Natural Benefics	Supportive forces of growth, grace, and harmony are more influential

Illustration C15C: Characteristics of Planets

A Story of Strength and Surrender

He looked at Vasudeva and softly said,

"You were born with Jupiter strong in the East, during the bright fortnight, in Uttarayana. That is not luck—that is a **celestial signature**. It tells me your strength lies in **sharing wisdom**, in lifting others, not through force, but **by simply being who you are**."

He turned his gaze to the disciples.

"Learn not just what planets you have—but **when they are strong**, and **how they want to move through you.** Only then will you not merely survive your chart—but dance with it."

Spiritual & Psychological Interpretation of Mandi in Cancer (2nd House)

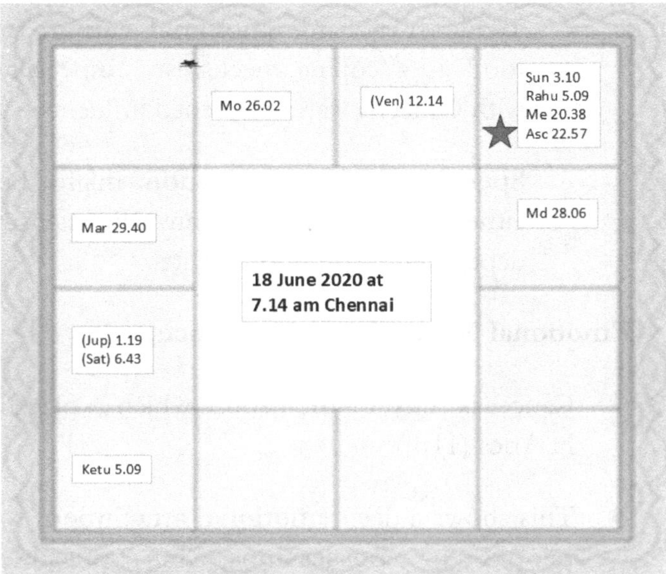

Illustration C1: Chart

2nd House – Speech, Values, Wealth, Food Habits

Mandi, a classical *upagraha* (shadow planet), is often linked to **illusions, delays, and karmic stagnation**.

- In the 2nd house, it can manifest as:
    - **Karmic patterns in speech** — needing purification or mindfulness in how one speaks.

  - Possible **difficulties with early family life or finances** that require endurance.
  - Tendency toward **emotional eating**, or food as a coping mechanism (especially with Cancer's water-elemental influence).
  - **Speech or communication** might be either overly reserved or unusually intense, depending on emotional state.

Emotional Tone (Cancer Influence)

- Cancer is ruled by the **Moon**, which is placed in Aries (11th).
- This shows a deep **emotional attachment to people or possessions**, but **possible difficulty expressing it clearly** due to Mandi's influence.

Guruji said:

"This Mandi brings a lesson — to master the art of restraint in speech, to treat words as sacred vibrations. What is withheld today returns tomorrow with wisdom."

Summary of the Chart's Essence

This is a chart filled with **intellectual brilliance, artistic grace, emotional complexity, and karmic depth.**

House	Sign	Planets / Upagrahas
1st (Lagna)	Gemini	Sun (3°10′), Rahu (5°09′), Mercury (20°38′), Asc (22°57′)
2nd	Cancer	Mandi (28°06′)
3rd	Leo	— (No planets)
4th	Virgo	— (No planets)
5th	Libra	— (No planets)
6th	Scorpio	— (No planets)
7th	Sagittarius	Ketu (5°09′)
8th	Capricorn	Jupiter (1°19′ R), Saturn (6°43′ R)
9th	Aquarius	Mars (29°40′)
10th	Pisces	— (No planets)
11th	Aries	Moon (26°02′)
12th	Taurus	Venus (12°14′ R – Retrograde)

Illustration C15D: Characteristics of Planets

Strengths:

- Mercury in its own sign = genius-level thinking, refined speech.
- Moon in 11th = popularity, emotional gains, joy through community.
- Venus (own sign, 12th) = spiritually elevated aesthetics, love for solitude.

- Jupiter + Saturn (8th) = hidden depth, mysticism, resilience through hardship.

Key Spiritual Themes:

- **Rahu-Sun in Lagna** = Ego purification, leadership journey.
- **Ketu in 7th** = Soulmate karma, detachment in relationships.
- **Mars in 9th** = Fierce dharma protector, spiritual courage.
- **Mandi in 2nd** = Voice of karma, learning when to speak and when to be still.

Ritus and the Planets: The Celestial Breath of Seasons

The afternoon sun filtered gently through the stone-latticed windows of the Buddha Hall, casting soft golden patterns on the floor like blessings laid in silence. The disciples, with their eyes lifted toward Guruji, whose presence felt both timeless and completely here.

The topic that day had moved from stars and planets to something more earthly — yet no less divine.

Padma, her voice like water over stone, asked softly,

"Guruji, we speak of the planets and their effects on life. But what of the seasons? Do the Ritus not speak the language of the grahas?"

"Ah," Guruji said, "the Ritus are the breathing of the Earth — and just as each breath is shaped by emotion, so too is each season shaped by a planet's touch. The Ritus are not random cycles. They are the Earth's six sacred moods, inspired by the cosmic dance of the grahas."

He leaned forward slightly and began, not as a teacher, but as a storyteller speaking to the winds.

Ritu (Season)	Planet	Natural Symbolism	Emotional/Spiritual Insight
Vasanta (Spring)	Venus	Blossoming flowers, vibrant colors, gentle warmth	Renewal, beauty, joy, creative awakening
Greeshma (Summer)	Mars	Intense heat, blazing sun, drought	Endurance, willpower, purification through effort
Varsha (Rainy)	Moon	Rain clouds, overflowing rivers, lush greenery	Emotional release, inner tides, nurturing, surrender
Hemanta (Dewy)	Mercury	Crisp mornings, clear skies, subtle transition	Intellectual clarity, balance, mindful reflection
Seeta (Winter)	Jupiter	Stillness, cold air, long nights, quiet Earth	Wisdom, inner grounding, study, retreat
Sisira (Fall)	Saturn	Falling leaves, bare trees, dry wind	Letting go, maturity, simplicity, detachment

Illustration C16A: Characteristics of Planets

1. Vasanta Ritu – Spring – Governed by Venus

"Spring is the season when the Earth blushes," he said, drawing an invisible lotus in the air. "Vasanta Ritu is ruled by Shukra – Venus, the planet of beauty, love, and harmony. When Venus breathes into the land, flowers bloom, colours return, and desire awakens—not lust, but the desire to live, to create, to feel again."

He looked at Abhirami, the artist, and said,

"In this season, even silence wears garlands. It is the return of softness after the trials of winter. The soul remembers how to dance."

2. Greeshma Ritu – Summer – Governed by Mars

"Then comes Greeshma, the season of fire and will, ruled by Mangala – Mars. This is not the gentle awakening of spring — this is intensity, the test of endurance. The Sun grows bold, rivers shrink, and everything living must prove its resilience."

He turned to Akshaya, whose nature was one of quiet strength.

"Mars teaches through heat. Summer is the battlefield where laziness burns and only clarity survives. It is the season of action, discipline, and transformation. Not everything survives the flame — but what does, emerges purified."

3. Varsha Ritu – Rainy Season – Governed by the Moon

Guruji paused as thunder rumbled faintly in the distance — as if Nature herself wanted to speak.

"And then, like a sigh after fire, comes the monsoon — Varsha Ritu, ruled by Chandra – the Moon. The parched Earth drinks deeply. Emotions rise like swollen rivers. The clouds cry, and the trees rejoice."

He looked toward Padma, whose empathy often welled like monsoon pools.

"This is the season of feeling, of release, of surrender. The Moon doesn't rush — it flows. And so, in this Ritu, we are invited to feel everything we had stored away in the heat. Joy. Grief. Memory. Longing. It is a season of the inner tide."

4. Hemanta Ritu – Dewy Pre-Winter – Governed by Mercury

"As the rains withdraw," Guruji continued, "comes the quiet dew of Hemanta, ruled by Budha – Mercury. The mind clears. The air sharpens. There is a balance between warmth and chill. This is the season of logic, of thought, of small joys — the rustle of dry leaves, the clarity of a morning walk."

He turned to Vidyarthi, the quiet learner.

"Mercury's Ritu doesn't scream. It whispers truths through reflection and dialogue. It is the season of inner understanding — a time when wisdom is not taught, but heard."

5. Seeta Ritu – Deep Winter – Governed by Jupiter

"Then arrives the hush of Seeta Ritu — winter, governed by Guru – Jupiter. This is the season of stillness, of wisdom sleeping in the roots. It is not dead — it is deeply alive within."

Guruji gestured upward, toward the silent peepal branches.

"Jupiter teaches us that growth does not always look like movement. In winter, things deepen. This is the time for study, for prayer, for stability. A tree may seem bare, but its sap is preparing its next offering."

To Sujitha, he smiled and said,

"You understand this. Winter is the season of the quiet teacher."

6. Sisira Ritu – Autumn – Governed by Saturn

"And finally, comes Sisira Ritu, the dry twilight between life and rebirth — governed by Shani – Saturn. This is the season of letting go. Leaves fall. Fields empty. The Earth prepares to shed."

He looked directly at Vasudeva, who had known personal loss but carried it with grace.

"Saturn does not arrive with cruelty, but with **truth.** Sisira teaches detachment, simplicity, and humility. It asks: *What are you ready to release? What no longer serves your journey?*"

The Hidden Cycle: Ritus Within Us

Guruji, after a pause, said.

"These six Ritus are not just outside you. They are within you. Your body experiences them. Your emotions mimic them. Your spiritual path moves through them."

Ritu (Season)	Colour	Dominant Dosha	Astrological Practices
Vasanta (Spring)	Pastel pink, green	Kapha	Chant Shukra Beej Mantra, wear light fabrics, practice acts of beauty & giving
Greeshma (Summer)	Red, orange	Pitta	Offer water to Sun, avoid anger, rise early, recite Hanuman Chalisa
Varsha (Rainy)	Silver, white	Kapha + Vata	Moon meditation, fasting on Mondays, strengthen emotional health, Chandra mantra
Hemanta (Dewy)	Green, pale yellow	Vata	Journal your thoughts, chant Budha mantra, wear green, communicate mindfully
Seeta (Winter)	Yellow, saffron	Vata + Kapha	Chant Guru mantra, study sacred texts, seek teacher's guidance
Sisira (Autumn)	Indigo, black	Vata	Practice detachment, perform Shani remedies, visit temples on Saturdays

Illustration C16B: Characteristics of Planets

He raised his hand and whispered,

"Every soul is a garden touched by these six winds. Venus brings the bloom, Mars tests the roots, the Moon waters the soil, Mercury sharpens the leaf, Jupiter strengthens the bark, and Saturn invites the leaves to fall — so that the cycle may begin again."

The Sacred Season You Are In

"Wherever you are in your journey, you are in some Ritu of the soul. Maybe spring, maybe autumn. It doesn't matter. What matters is that you honour it — live it fully, feel it deeply, and know that the grahas are not watching from above…

…they are **growing within you.**"

And in that moment, the hall felt like a living forest, and the disciples like trees — each one swaying softly in the rhythm of the Ritus… listening to their **planetary season** unfold.

Evening Break Under the Banyan Tree – A Story of Stillness and Stars

As the evening sun leaned gently toward the western horizon, the golden light softened, casting long shadows across the quiet grounds of the ashram. The birds, like scattered thoughts finally returning home, fluttered back to their nests with whispers of the sky folded in their wings.

A stillness settled over the land — not silence, but something deeper: a kind of sacred hush.

From the Buddha Hall, **Guruji**, with his timeless grace, smiled and said in his soothing voice,

"Now, let us pause. The body must rest so the soul may absorb. Go… breathe with the trees. Feel the rhythm of dusk. We shall meet again after the sun has offered its final bow."

And so, the disciples stepped out like petals from a lotus — quietly, reverently.

The Gathering Beneath the Banyan

Beneath the ancient **banyan tree**, whose aerial roots dangled like the threads of ancestral memory, a small circle began to form.

Kiran, Sam, Alice, Sofia, Bhavya, Aarna, Dev, and John each found their place under its protective canopy. Some sat on the stone platform, others on the cool grass. Their faces bore the afterglow of the day's teachings — open, softened, quietly alive.

Soon, from the direction of the ashram kitchen, came the comforting aroma of freshly brewed coffee and chai.

Padma, ever graceful, carried a tray with mud cups, her hands steady like her gaze. Akshaya followed, handing cups gently, as if offering sacred blessings. Vasudeva, with his warm silence, simply smiled and poured — his service was his speech.

The first sips brought warmth not just to the hands, but to the heart. The evening air carried the scent of Tulsi and wet earth. Somewhere far off, a conch shell had just sounded.

Apeksha's Story: The Star That Waited

As the group fell into a natural rhythm of quiet chatter, Apeksha, who had been watching the sky with her usual contemplative stillness, finally spoke.

Her voice was low, but it carried — like a flute note that cuts through even the deepest silence.

"Do you know," she began, "there is a story the stars once told me… about a star who never rose."

Everyone turned toward her, even the wind.

"It is said that there was once a star — not the brightest, not the boldest — just a small star, tucked near the edge of the sky. Every evening, it would wait… hoping to rise, to shine, to be seen.

But every time it was prepared, a cloud would come. Or the moon would steal the scene. Or the night would pass too quickly. 'Not yet,' said Time. 'Not now,' whispered the heavens.

And still, the star waited. It learned to watch others shine. It learned to celebrate silently. It learned to hold its light — not for applause, but because it was light.

And then, one night, when no one was watching, when even the moon was sleeping behind the hills, the sky opened — utterly still — and the star rose. Quietly. Beautifully.

It didn't dazzle. It didn't command. But the night remembered.

Because it was the star that had waited… and waiting had made it pure."

Her words settled over the group like evening dew — cool, glistening, soft. A deep stillness followed, but not the kind that demanded words. It was the kind that made you want to close your eyes and feel what's inside.

Kiran's Sigh and the Return to Silence

As the sky above turned from amber to indigo, Kiran, who had been tracing the story in the folds of his breath, let out a soft sigh.

"It's time," he said, not with urgency, but with reverence.

The others stood slowly, cradling the last warmth of their cups, their hearts just a little fuller than before.

They began to walk back toward the Buddha Hall, each carrying a quiet part of the star's story — a light that didn't demand to be seen, but chose to wait until it was truly needed.

The banyan tree, the eternal witness, stood still behind them, its shadow stretching across the earth like a prayer.

And above, somewhere in the vastness of night, a small star blinked — not to be noticed,

but to remind the sky that light…

even when unseen,

still shines.

CHAPTER IV

The Mystical Attributes IV

"The planets do not merely rule the stars — they breathe through the roots beneath our feet, the metals we shape, and the pulse within every living being. In Jeeva, Moola, and Dhatu, the cosmos reveals its earthly reflection."— Shree Shambav.

Jeeva, Moola, and Dhatu

The sun had fully set, and the Buddha Hall was cloaked in the soft hush of twilight. The devotees gathered once more, refreshed from their evening break under the banyan tree. The fragrance of jasmine mingled with the faint scent of camphor. A hush fell across the room as Guruji entered.

He took his seat with a grace that stilled even the wind. After a moment of silence — as if the cosmos was waiting for him to speak — he began: "Just as all of creation can be divided into earth, water, fire, air, and ether," he said, "so too can all that exists — living, growing, or inanimate — be classified as Jeeva, Moola, and Dhatu.

These are not merely categories… they are the three strands of manifestation through which the planets whisper their will into the world."

Category	Meaning	Governing Planets	Symbolic Insight
Jeeva	Living beings, vitality	Ketu, Jupiter, Mercury	Represents the breath of life, consciousness, instinct, intelligence
Moola	Roots and vegetables	Sun, Venus	Symbolises nourishment, sensual growth, grounded beauty
Dhatu	Metals, minerals, inanimate matter	Rahu, Mars, Saturn, Moon	Reflects form, endurance, material structure, and emotional memory (Moon)

Illustration C17A: Characteristics of Planets

Moola – The Pulse of the Soil

Guruji leaned forward slightly and gestured to a small brass bowl of tulsi roots on the altar.

"Moola means roots — the carriers of life that remain hidden beneath the surface, yet feed all growth. These are the vegetables, the herbs, the things that take nourishment from the womb of the earth. They are ruled by the Sun and Venus."

He paused, letting the imagery take root in the minds of the disciples.

"The Sun, being the source of life, gives these roots vitality. And Venus, with her sweetness and refinement, gives them flavour, nourishment, and beauty. Together, they bless what we consume from the soil with both strength and pleasure."

He smiled at Bhavya, who had earlier spoken of starting a small herbal garden.

"If you plant carrots, turmeric, or beetroot — do it when the Sun rises strong or Venus shines clear. Your garden will then carry the signature of cosmic harmony."

Dhatu – The Bones of the World

He then picked up a small iron trident from beside him.

"Next, there is Dhatu — the metals, minerals, and materials that build form and strength. These are the bones of the world — the skeleton of Shiva, if you will."

"Rahu, Mars, Saturn, and the Moon govern these elements. Why such a curious mix? Because materials are both tough and temperamental. Mars gives them force, Saturn endurance, Rahu the shadow of transformation, and the Moon — surprisingly — gives them adaptability, their changing quality under heat, light, or touch."

He looked toward Dev, who worked with sculpture.

"When you forge metal, choose your time wisely. If Saturn is exalted, your creation will last lifetimes. If Rahu is dominant, it may shimmer with mystery — but handle with care. Dhatus remember the moods of the cosmos."

Category	Examples / Applications	Ideal Planetary Influence
Jeeva	Animals, humans, livestock, bees, organic movement or health-related projects	Strong Jupiter, Mercury, or Ketu periods for new life, healing, or education
Moola	Root crops (carrot, beetroot, turmeric), herbs, Ayurveda, farming	Plant or harvest during strong Sun or Venus transit or Dasha
Dhatu	Iron, copper tools, sculptures, building materials, ornaments	Choose Mars or Saturn periods for construction; Rahu for innovation

Illustration C17B: Characteristics of Planets

Jeeva – The Breath That Moves

Guruji's tone grew gentler, more reverent.

"And then… we come to Jeeva — the living ones. The creatures that breathe, crawl, fly, and speak. This is the domain of the divine spark — of soul-stuff. And it is governed by Ketu, Jupiter, and Mercury."

A few disciples looked surprised. Guruji noticed and smiled.

"Why Ketu?" he asked rhetorically. "Because Ketu governs the unseen intelligence of life — the instincts, the karmic memory within the DNA.

Jupiter nourishes them — he is the Guru, the guide, the spirit of growth. And Mercury gives movement, expression, cognition — he is the breath between thought and action."

He gestured toward Alice, who raised bees in her hometown.

"If you bring bees into your garden, or even tend to the sick, check these planets. A strong Jupiter brings thriving; a quiet Mercury may cause miscommunication. A shadowed Ketu can indicate that karmic healing is required before peace returns."

A Garden of Threefold Blessing

Apeksha, who had been quietly observing, softly added:

"Guruji, your words remind me of an old woman in my village. She tended a garden not for food, but for prayer. In one corner, she grew roots — turmeric, ginger — during Venus hours.

In another, she planted iron bells and copper pots among her basil plants, always after Saturn's darshan.

And she fed the birds and goats that came, always on a Thursday, when Jupiter's blessings were strongest.

Her garden wasn't big. But nothing there ever fell sick. Her plants were never eaten by insects. The birds returned every season. It was as if… the cosmos itself was keeping watch."

Guruji closed his eyes briefly and whispered,

"Because she wasn't gardening the soil… she was gardening her **karma**."

Alignment is Devotion

"So remember," Guruji said, "everything you touch belongs to a graha.

If you walk in tune with them — whether growing roots, forging iron, or nursing a life — your work becomes prayer, and your world becomes temple."

How Your Rasi Evolves You

Outside, a gentle breeze stirred the neem leaves, and within, a deep stillness settled — not just of silence, but of expectancy. The kind of stillness that comes when something timeless is about to be said.

Akshatha, ever curious and wide-eyed, leaned slightly forward, her notebook poised on her lap. That evening, the question she asked had lingered in the air long after her voice had fallen quiet:

"Guruji, why do I feel like I've become a completely different person over the years? Am I changing, or just understanding myself more?"

Guruji looked at her, his gaze soft yet penetrating — like moonlight passing through water.

He smiled and began, his voice woven with wisdom, pause, and poetry.

The Rasi and the River of Time

Guruji said, "We do not remain the same, even though we wear the same name. A soul walks through life like a river through shifting valleys. And though the river flows from the same source, each bend changes it."

"Your Rasi, your zodiac sign — it is the Moon's home at the moment of your birth. It reflects your emotional blueprint, your instinctual self, your inner tides. But like the Moon, your Rasi does not remain still. It travels through time's great loom, weaving new shades into your soul."

Dashas: The Decades that Redefine You

"Life," Guruji continued, "is divided not by age alone, but by Dashas — planetary periods that mark the rhythm of your evolution. Each Dasha is like a new teacher entering your classroom of destiny. Some are gentle, like Venus, bringing beauty and love. Others, like Ketu, are fierce — stripping you bare, so you may find your true skin."

He turned to Sudharshan, who had recently entered his Shani Dasha, and said:

"Even if you are a Scorpio by birth, under Saturn's gaze, your Mars-born intensity may give way to a quiet endurance. That is not a contradiction, Akshatha — that is refinement."

The Sculptor Saturn and the Sadesati

Then he paused, eyes turning distant — not in forgetfulness, but remembrance.

"Let me tell you a story," he said, "of a potter and a lump of clay."

"Once, a potter picked up a strange lump of earth. It was stubborn, unyielding, and full of pride. But the potter smiled, and began his work. First, he softened it with water — this was the early joy of life. Then, he spun it rapidly, dizzying it with turns of fate. Finally, he placed it in the fire — not to destroy it, but to strengthen it.

That fire is Sadesati — the seven-and-a-half-year period when Saturn transits over your Moon sign, your

Rasi. It humbles. It hardens. It heals. And when you emerge from it, you are "not broken — you are cured."

He turned back to Akshatha, his voice gentle now:

"If you feel you have changed every decade, it is because you have. The stars never intended for you to remain untouched."

The Growing Tree of Personality

"Think of yourself as a tree," he continued, "and your Rasi as your seed code. A mango tree cannot bear lemons — but even a mango tree begins as a seed, becomes a sapling, then a trunk, and bears fruit. Your early decades may show only the raw wood of your Sun or Mars, but later you may flower under Mercury's reason or Venus's grace."

"An Aries child may be impulsive and fearless. But that same Aries, after a Saturn period, becomes strategic — not because their fire has died, but because it has found direction."

Careers, Relationships, and Shifting Soul Directions

"And so too," Guruji said, "do our desires, relationships, and dharmas evolve. A child drawn to conquest may one day long for service. A lover of luxury may become a seeker of silence. These are not betrayals of your Rasi — they are its unfolding."

He looked toward Ramya, who had once been a banker and now taught at a small school.

"She did not abandon her chart — she understood it more deeply."

The Rasi Is Not a Prison — It Is a Portal

As the night grew deeper, the room felt less like a hall and more like a womb — warm, sacred, still.

Guruji stood, slowly.

"So remember, Akshatha… your Rasi is not your cage. It is your beginning. And with each decade, with each Dasha, with each passing of Saturn's gaze — you do not become someone else.

You become more yourself."

"If you ever wonder why, you no longer laugh the way you did at 20, or love the way you did at 30, or dream the way you did at 40 — it is not because you have lost your way. It is because you are walking it… and the stars, ever so gently, are teaching you how to become."

Shree Shambavaya Namaha (Invoking the Divine—the ever-transforming, ever-still essence of time and timelessness.)

Navigating Decadal Changes: A Journey Through Time and Soul

Imagine life as a vast river—majestic, unpredictable, winding through valleys of youth and over the cliffs of age. Each decade is like a different stretch of that river. Some sections are calm and reflective, others are turbulent, rushing with the force of unseen currents. The Rasi (your Moon sign) and the Dasha (planetary period) are the winds and celestial tides that shape these waters. You are the boatman—and self-awareness is your oar.

Self-Awareness: The Sacred Compass Within

To understand the transformation that each decade brings, one must journey inward. This is where the ancient science of Vedic astrology becomes not merely a system, but a mirror to the soul. Your Rasi, determined by the position of the Moon at the time of your birth, is not just a sign—it is the archetype of your inner world, your emotional rhythm, your subconscious response to the world.

Overlay this with the planetary Dashas—periods ruled by different planets that govern our karma—and you have a cosmic blueprint of your evolving self.

The First Decade: The Seedling Stage

Like a sprout pushing through the soil, we are shaped by the Moon's influence in our early years—sensitive, reactive, and absorbing impressions like water. Here, Chandra's gentle, nurturing touch can make us cling to the known, while Mars may make us impulsive and bold. If our Dasha lord is harsh, early challenges become the chisel that carves character.

The Second and Third Decades: The Furnace of Fire

In our teens and twenties, the fire of planets like Mars, Rahu, or the Sun may dominate—ushering periods of ambition, chaos, or identity crisis. One may feel split between what the soul desires and what the world demands. This is the time when illusions begin to crack. The river of life may crash into unseen rocks. This is when knowing your Rasi and Dasha becomes not just helpful, but essential.

Knowing, for example, that Saturn's Mahadasha has begun might explain the sense of delay, pressure, or isolation—urging you to slow down, to develop discipline, to shed the false and embrace solitude. Without such awareness, these changes may feel cruel. With it, they become sacred.

Remedies and Adjustments: Aligning with the Celestial Dharma

Not all storms can be stopped—but their intensity can be softened.

Vedic astrology doesn't just diagnose your planetary condition—it offers prescriptions to harmonise with it. The ancients knew that energy must be balanced, and if cosmic forces are misaligned, we must act.

Rituals & Mantras

Chanting the name of the Dasha lord—be it "Om Namo Bhagavate Vasudevaya" for Jupiter or "Om Sham Shanicharaya Namaha" for Saturn—can tune your inner vibration with cosmic resonance.

Gemstones

Like tuning forks for the soul, gemstones carry the essence of planetary energy. Wearing a Blue Sapphire during Saturn's period (if it suits your chart) can ground you and provide resilience. But only with guidance, for the same gem can bless or bruise, depending on your karmic path.

Spiritual Practices

Above all, practices like meditation, seva (selfless service), and mantra sadhana offer the deepest transformation. These aren't mere tools—they are paths. As the Gita says, "He who sees inaction in action, and action in inaction, is wise among men." The true remedy is not escape—it is alignment.

The Phoenix Analogy: Death and Rebirth Every Decade

Think of each decade like the life cycle of a Phoenix. At the end of each ten-year stretch, the person you once were burns in the fire of experience—a death not of body, but of identity. Out of those ashes, a new you is born—wiser, wearier, but also more wondrous. The Rasi determines what kind of Phoenix you are, while the Dashas determine how often and how deeply you must burn and rise again.

So if you find yourself lost, uncertain, or uprooted at the turn of a decade—it may not be a crisis. It may be the birth pangs of your next self. The stars are not cursing you. They are sculpting you.

Embracing the Flow of Destiny

Just as the river does not resist the rocks, but carves beauty from them, your soul is shaped by the very forces that challenge it. The Rasi is your original script, and the Dashas are the directors who stage your play. But you are not merely an actor. With self-awareness, you become the co-writer. With remedies, you become the healer. With faith, you become the flame that dances in the dark.

And through every decade, you do not merely change—you become. You become closer to who you truly are. You become the essence behind the form.

You become... Shambav— The one who transforms, yet remains eternal.

Shree Shambavaya Namaha … Let the dance of time be your teacher, let the light of self-knowledge be your guide.

The Gathering Flame

The Buddha Hall fell into a contemplative hush as Guruji, after a long, thoughtful pause, quietly folded his hands and stepped away, drawing the day's discourse to a close. His silence echoed louder than words, carrying the gravity of the evening's teachings. The devotees, still swimming in the depths of inner reflection, rose slowly—each person reluctant to break the spell of that silence.

Outside, the night had woven a tapestry of serenity. The breeze was cool and wrapped around the skin like a silken shawl. Nocturnal creatures hummed their unseen songs, as though the forest itself had entered a meditative chant. The moon, suspended like a lamp of calm awareness, cast silver trails across the earth, while stars twinkled above like the blinking eyes of celestial sages, bearing silent witness to the soul's quiet awakening.

As the last stragglers left the hall, Padma stood still for a moment, absorbing the weight of the evening, then softly said, "Let us gather near the fire after dinner." There was no debate—only nods. As if her words were already part of some unsaid tradition.

An Hour Later – The Fire Circle

The fire crackled gently, a dancing oracle of orange and gold, speaking in a language older than words. Around it sat Sam, Alice, Sofia, Bhavya, Aarna, Dev, and John—each one cloaked not just in shawls, but in questions, memories, and quiet awe. Their voices murmured over one another in soft discussion, the way rivers merge and flow together.

Soon, Akshaya arrived with her quiet grace, followed by Padma, serene as always. Nita's laughter preceded her, Lalitha's silence followed like a shadow, and Rohith came, half lost in thought, half drawn by the warmth of companionship. Others drifted in, drawn not by invitation, but by some instinctive pull—like migratory birds finding their flock.

The fire became the centre—not just of warmth, but of presence.

As was custom, Kieron turned to Apeksha. "Tell us something," he said. "Something that touches not just the mind, but the marrow."

Apeksha smiled. Not the smile of one who performs, but of one who has wandered long through the labyrinths of life and returned with treasures.

She began.

The Forgotten Shrine

High in the timeless folds of the Himalayas, where the wind speaks in whispers of eternity and the mountains carry the weight of both snow and silence, there lived a young seeker named Aarav.

He had left behind the world of noise and names—family, ambition, even the comforts of identity—in search of something that words could not contain. Enlightenment. Truth. God. Not the God of rituals or scriptures, but the still, unnameable essence behind all things.

At first, the mountains welcomed him. The silence was a balm, the snow a teacher. He meditated at dawn and dusk, chanted mantras through the long, icy nights, and fasted until his body felt like breath and bone. Years passed. The seasons turned like prayer wheels.

But the Divine remained silent.

No visions. No celestial voices. Not even a flicker of bliss.

Instead, the cold grew colder. The silence, once sacred, now felt suffocating. His inner world, once ripe with devotion, had turned into a barren landscape. Doubt began to trickle in like melting snow—slow, cold, and relentless.

"Have I been abandoned by the Divine?" "Or worse... has it all been a lie?"

One winter night, the wind howled like an unquiet spirit, and the moon hung low like an indifferent eye. Aarav sat outside his cave, shivering both from the cold and the ache in his heart. He looked out at the vast mountains—those majestic keepers of sages past—and something in him snapped.

With tears streaming down his sunken cheeks, he cried out, "Why? Why won't you come? Why this silence? Am I not worthy? Or are You simply not there?"

He fell to his knees. His voice cracked. He cursed the mountains—the very path he once revered. He beat his fists against the earth, against his own faith.

And then it happened.

The rock beneath his feet—loose from years of unnoticed erosion—gave way. Aarav stumbled backwards, flailing to catch himself. In the chaos, his hand struck something solid. Rough. Cold. Covered in moss. He turned, wiping tears from his eyes, and saw it.

A small shrine, carved crudely into the rock. Old, forgotten. Almost swallowed by the forest's slow embrace.

He gasped. It had been right there, perhaps just a few paces from where he meditated every day. He had passed it countless times, never noticing. It was modest, without grandeur—just a stone alcove with a worn image of Shiva inside, half-covered in snow.

And yet, in that moment, it radiated more presence than any temple he'd ever entered.

Aarav sank to his knees again—this time not in despair, but in reverence. The shrine hadn't appeared suddenly. It had always been there. He had simply been too consumed with looking outward, too fixated on a dramatic revelation, too attached to how the Divine should appear.

In his fall, something broke open—not his faith, but his false expectations.

And into that opening, Grace entered.

He closed his eyes, and for the first time in years, he did not search. He simply was.

And in that stillness, he felt it—not as a voice, not as a vision, but as an unshakable knowing:

What you seek is not hidden. It is only waiting for you to stop looking elsewhere. You were never alone. You simply forgot how to see.

The fire in him rekindled—not the fire of seeking, but of being.

The Teaching

When Apeksha finished narrating the story by the fire that night, a soft silence fell over the group. Not the silence of awkwardness—but the silence that follows a sudden remembering. As if everyone there had glimpsed a piece of themselves in Aarav.

The mountains in the story were not just geographical—they were metaphors for life's trials, spiritual ambitions, and illusions. And the shrine? That was the soul.

Hidden. Patient. Waiting not to be built—but to be noticed.

The Lamp of Varanasi

Her name was Meera, and she lived in a quiet corner of Varanasi, whcrc thc ghats meet the Ganga in eternal dialogue between life and death, faith and fire. Time in Varanasi did not move like it did elsewhere—it drifted like incense, slow and sacred, curling around stone temples, ash-smeared sadhus, and widows draped in white.

Meera had been a widow for many years now. Her husband, a humble teacher, had passed away when their only son, Arjun, was just six. From that moment, her world had narrowed into two anchors—her son and her devotion.

Each morning, before the first light touched the steps of the ghat, Meera would wake, bathe, and walk barefoot to the small temple near the peepal tree, carrying a brass diya—a lamp with cotton wicks dipped in ghee. It wasn't just ritual; it was a vow. A covenant of protection.

Every day, she whispered the same prayer into the flame:

"May my Arjun be safe. Let no harm come to him. Watch over him when I cannot."

She would light the lamp before the deity, bow her head, and stay a few moments longer—until the lamp steadied, and her breath calmed.

In the beginning, her prayers were frantic, desperate—a mother terrified of losing what little remained of her world. But over the years, they became quieter, more rhythmic—like a mantra the heart recited in its own language.

And she believed—deeply, unquestionably—that this small act held her world together.

The Forgotten Flame

Then, one monsoon morning, heavy with grey clouds and the ache of old bones, Meera overslept. The alarm bell of the temple gongs had already rung by the time she woke. Her body ached, her mind swirled in confusion. By the time she remembered the lamp—it was too late.

Panic gripped her like a cold hand. She sat in the centre of her small room, breathless. "I forgot. Oh God… I forgot."

All day, she waited for the storm. A letter. A knock on the door. A cry from the neighbours. She imagined Arjun—now grown and working in another city—struck by some unseen misfortune. A mother's mind, when unanchored, can become a theatre of terror.

But the day passed. And then another. And then a week.

No tragedy. No catastrophe. Arjun called as usual, his voice warm and cheerful. Nothing had crumbled.

One evening, Meera stood again before the lamp in the temple. She lit it slowly, with trembling hands—not from age, but from the tremor of realisation blooming inside her.

As the flame flickered to life, her eyes filled with tears—not of sorrow, but of release.

"You are not in the lamp," she whispered. "You are in the hands that lit it. In the love that moved those hands. In the breath that whispered those prayers. In the silence that stayed after the words ended."

She wept—not from fear, but from the soft breaking of an illusion. Not because she had lost faith, but because she had found something deeper.

Her God had not abandoned her. He had simply stepped out from the diya and revealed Himself in her own being.

When Apeksha ended the story, the fire around which they sat crackled softly, as if echoing the small flame of Meera's lamp—flickering but unbroken.

Padma, who had listened with her eyes closed, gently said,

"How often we mistake the shell for the source. We think Divine lives in the ritual—but forget He lives in the intent behind it."

And Sam added,

"Sometimes, only when we forget our devotion do we truly understand it."

Meera's story was not just about a mother. It was about all of us—those who light lamps of effort, habit, and prayer hoping to keep chaos at bay. It was about how control masquerades as faith, and how sometimes grace arrives not when we do everything right, but when we forget, when we fall, when we stop grasping—and discover that the Divine was never in the flame… but in us, all along.

The lamp had never held God. It had held her trust. And when that trust no longer needed a vessel, it became something vast and formless—like the Ganga beside her city. Ever flowing. Always sacred.

Both stories were simple—but like seeds, they carried whole forests inside.

As Apeksha spoke, even the flames seemed to still, and the forest held its breath. The stars above shone brighter—not in brilliance, but in intimacy—as if leaning closer, listening like old friends who had heard these truths before, and longed to hear them again.

The Gentle Unwinding

After a long, reverent silence, Kiran stretched, his voice heavy with sleep and soul, "The night has been long… and kind," he said. "Let's rest. Tomorrow will ask more of us."

One by one, they rose—not hurriedly, but with the slowness of those still wrapped in another world. Shawls drawn close, eyes half-lidded with dreams yet to form, they returned to their rooms—though none truly left the fire behind. It had lit something in them that would smoulder quietly through the night.

The moon climbed higher, and the forest resumed its rhythm. The fire burned low, but within each seeker, something burned brighter.

And the stars… The stars stayed. Watching. Listening. Remembering.

PART TWO

The Celestial Order

"The celestial order is not chaos tamed, but wisdom revealed—each star a syllable in the silent scripture of the divine, each orbit a rhythm in the sacred music of becoming."

- *Shree Shambav*

CHAPTER V

The Mask and the Mirror

"The ascendant is not the soul, but its silhouette at sunrise—what the world sees before it meets your shadow, your light, and the truth that lies beyond both."

Morning in the Buddha Hall: The Mirror of the Ascendant

The morning air was wrapped in a gentle coolness, the kind that holds the hush of dawn just a little longer. Soft beams of sunlight filtered through the carved wooden lattice of the Buddha Hall, painting golden patterns on the marble floor. Incense drifted lazily in the air, a silent offering of breath and stillness.

One by one, the devotees entered with quiet reverence—wrapped in shawls, silence, and expectancy. They settled, forming a sea of still presence. Murmurs faded. The soft rustling of robes ceased. A palpable calm spread through the hall, as though even the walls were holding their breath.

Then, Guruji entered.

His presence didn't stir the room like a gust of wind—it entered like the sun behind a cloud: soft, illuminating, undeniable.

He sat in silence.

The silence stretched—not awkwardly, but like a sacred bridge between yesterday's knowing and today's awakening.

Then, at last, Guruji's voice emerged—low, slow, and resonant, like the first notes of a raga at sunrise:

"Astrologers often examine the planets near your ascendant—your rising sign—to understand how you present yourself to the world. This ascendant... is not who you are in the depths of your soul. It is the door through which the world enters and the mirror through which it sees you."

A hush followed. He let the words land, like pebbles on the still surface of a pond.

The Ascendant: The First Veil

He continued, his voice like warm wind moving through ancient truths.

"Imagine your life is a house," he said. "The ascendant is not the innermost room of your soul. It is the front porch—the place where guests arrive. Before they know your heart, your fears, or your dreams, they meet your porch. And depending on which planet stands at that door, the world sees you differently."

He paused, scanning the room, as if to say: Now, listen with your heart.

Mars on the Ascendant – The Warrior at the Gate

"When Mars stands guard at your ascendant," Guruji said, "your porch is a battlefield, even if your soul is a temple. The world sees a warrior first—bold eyes, strong will, an energy that says 'Do not waste my time.'"

He leaned forward, eyes glinting with quiet intensity.

"Such a person walks into a room, and people feel the air shift—decisiveness, clarity, purpose. But that strength... if not balanced, can become a sword drawn too quickly. Mars gives fire, yes—but fire can light a home or burn it down."

He looked toward a young man in the front row—eyes wide, back straight.

"You may carry Mars in your bones," he said gently. "But remember... even a warrior must sometimes lay down his armour to truly connect."

Venus on the Ascendant – The Flowering Garden

Guruji then closed his eyes briefly, as if invoking the spirit of another planet.

"And when Venus graces the ascendant… Ah, then your porch is a garden in bloom. The world meets fragrance before it meets the fruit. Beauty before depth. You offer ease, charm, warmth—people are drawn to you not because of fear, but because of comfort."

He smiled softly, his voice like a gentle breeze.

"But even this can become a mask. When you are always pleasing, always soft, where does your true strength live? Venus teaches connection, but also boundaries. Kindness... without losing your soul's direction."

He turned to an elderly woman whose face seemed carved with grace and long years.

"You carry Venus," he said, "but even roses grow thorns. That, too, is part of love."

The Teaching: The Mask and the Mirror

He sat back, letting the teachings settle. Then, with a voice both gentle and piercing, he concluded:

"The ascendant is not the soul's truth. But it is the first language the world understands. Knowing it is not a vanity—it is a form of self-awareness. It is the mirror you offer to the world.

But remember: mirrors reflect light only when turned toward it. The planets near your ascendant shape how you begin—but not where you end."

The Stillness After

The devotees sat in profound silence, not because they had nothing to say, but because something within them had just been named—a part of themselves long known, now finally seen.

Outside, the morning sun had climbed higher. Birds sang softly in the peepul trees. And within each listener, the flame of self-understanding had been quietly lit.

CHAPTER VI

The Symphony of Subtle Forces

When Planets Speak Through Colour, Taste, and Stone

Guruji said, "Let us now delve deeper—not into the stars above—but into how those stars speak through the materials of the Earth itself… through metals, colours, tastes, grains, and gems. These are not mere preferences of culture or chance. They are echoes. Echoes of the planets that influence your life from the moment of your first breath."

The Earth Remembers the Sky

He looked around the room, letting his words breathe.

"You see, we are not just bodies moving through space. We are vessels of cosmic memory. Just as a conch shell carries the sound of the ocean it once belonged to, each of us carries within us the whisper of planetary energies. And these whispers surface... in the metals we wear, the colours that soothe us, the tastes we crave when we're lost, the foods that comfort us, the stones that seem to glow only when they touch our skin."

He paused, then said with a smile,

"The stars don't just shine in the sky. They shine through your choices."

The Planets and Their Earthly Signatures

"The Sun," he said, "governs gold, red hues, the taste of pungency, and the grain wheat. To wear gold is to carry the sun's fire on your body. It strengthens the heart, uplifts your spirit. But not everyone can hold the sun directly—it must be earned, like confidence born of clarity. The gem of the Sun is ruby—the stone of kings, meant for those who must lead with heart and light."

He turned toward a young woman named Rekha at the front.

"You are drawn to gold not because it is precious, but because your inner sun has been dimmed. The metal reminds you of the fire within that still waits to rise."

"The Moon," he continued, "rules silver, white and pale blue, the taste of salty comfort, and the grain rice. Silver is lunar wisdom—cool, reflective, nurturing. Its energy calms storms, within and without. Its gem is a pearl, not forged by fire, but by the soft resistance of life to pain. A tear hardened into light."

He glanced at a young man whose fingers nervously fidgeted.

"You wear a silver ring," Guruji observed. "Not as decoration, but as a promise of emotional balance. Let it remind you: what feels heavy now is but a wave passing through."

"Mars," he said next, "claims copper, the bold reds and scarlets, the sharp taste of spice, and the grain masoor dal. It is energy incarnate—raw, ready, relentless. The gem is red coral, a stone not of the sky, but of the sea's untamed blood. Mars is fire you must learn to tame, not extinguish."

He turned to a man sitting tall, his jaw set like stone.

"Your Mars burns too close to the skin. Let the spice be in your will, not your words. Coral will help—not to cage your fire, but to anchor it."

And so he moved through the planets, each like a chapter in a living scripture:

Mercury with emerald, the colour green, the taste of bitterness, and grains like green gram, enhancing intellect and adaptability.

Jupiter, the priest-planet, with yellow sapphire, the taste of sweetness, turmeric, and the grain chana dal—inviting wisdom, growth, and expansion.

Venus, sensual and artistic, favoring diamond, white tones, sugars, and luxury grains like fine rice.

Saturn, the great karmic teacher, is linked to iron, black and blue, the taste of astringency, and coarse grains like urad dal—reminding one of endurance, patience, and discipline.

The Story Within

Guruji said, "Let me narrate a story: Long ago, in a kingdom forgotten by history but remembered by the stars, there lived a blind sage. He could not see the sky—but he could feel the vibration of planets through the metals he held, the grains he touched, and the gems he placed in water before drinking. Once, a young prince came to him, lost and torn between duty and desire. The sage gave him a simple necklace of copper and coral and said, 'This will not give you answers. But it will give you the strength to hear them when they come.' The prince wore it through war and peace, until one day, he no longer needed it. Not because the energy had faded—but because it had fully awakened within him."

Guruji looked out into the room, his voice now a whisper of thunder:

"What you wear on your body, you eventually grow within your spirit. The planets offer tools—not as destiny, but as keys. Keys to unlock balance, power, and presence."

The Earth remembers the stars. And through colour, taste, texture, and tone—the heavens speak.

Whispered by the Stars – Planetary Insight with Guruji

Guruji seated himself on the raised platform. He took a sip of tulsi water, closed his eyes briefly, then opened them—his gaze warm, deep, and full of recognition.

"Now," he said, "let the questions come—not from the mind alone, but from the soul that aches to understand its path."

Bhavya asked, "Guruji… I feel pulled in two directions—towards responsibility, and towards an unknown longing for something greater. I feel like my life is split. Why?"

Guruji smiled gently.

"This is the voice of Saturn and Jupiter within you. Saturn pulls you towards duty, structure, and the weight of karma. Jupiter whispers of expansion, purpose, and the soul's search for meaning. The split is not a mistake—it is a dance. Saturn teaches you to walk the earth. Jupiter reminds you to look at the sky while walking."

He paused.

"Wear a simple iron ring to ground your Saturn. But also keep a yellow cloth near your altar. It will remind you of your dharma—your higher calling. You are not split—you are being sculpted."

Bhavya folded her hands, tears falling like blessings from eyes that had been clouded for too long.

Planet	Metal	Colour	Taste	Grains	Gems
Sun	Gold / Copper	Blood-red Hue/ Saffron	Pungent	Wheat	Ruby
Moon	Silver / Bell metal	White / Tawny shade	Saltish	Rice	Spotless Pearl
Mars	Copper	Blood-red	Bitter	Dhal	Coral
Mercury	Ore / Bronze	Grass Green	Mixed	Green Gram	Emerald
Jupiter	Gold	Yellow/ Tawny tone	Sweet	Bengal Gram	Yellow sapphire
Venus	Silver	White/ Multiple colour	Sour	Cow gram	Diamond
Saturn	Iron	Black	Astringent	Seasame	Sapphire
Rahu	Tin	Dark blue and ultraviolet	Bitter and pungent	Black gram	Gomedha
Ketu	Bronze	Earthy and smoky tones	Spicy and sharp flavours	Horse gram	Cats Eye

Illustration PMCT2: Various aspect governed by different planets.

Sam, ever the sceptic, leaned in next.

Sam: "Guruji, I've never believed in planetary influence. I make my own choices. Why should Mars or Mercury decide my fate?"

Guruji looked at him with no judgment—only calm curiosity.

"The planets do not decide your fate, Sam. They reveal the currents within your own ocean. You still choose the boat, the sail, and the direction. But if Mars stirs high tides in your temperament, wouldn't you want to know before setting out?"

He continued:

"Your sharp tongue, your impatience, your drive—they are not flaws. They are Mars rising within you. Offer water to the Sun on Tuesday mornings. Touch copper with gratitude. Channel that fire into service, not conflict."

Sam blinked, as if something had quietly landed in him he couldn't yet name.

Sofia, among them, asked in a soft voice:

Sofia: "Guruji, I feel emotions too deeply. I absorb people's moods. It overwhelms me. Is this also… planetary?"

Guruji nodded gently.

"You, carry a strong Moon and perhaps Venus near your ascendant. Your heart is a harp—beautiful, but sensitive to every touch of wind. This is a gift. But even a harp needs a case when not played."

He leaned forward slightly, his voice kind and protective.

"Wear silver, especially on Mondays. Keep a pearl close to your skin. Eat warm, soothing foods. Let your creativity be your filter, not your burden."

Sofia smiled through her tears. For the first time, her sensitivity felt like a sacred design, not a personal flaw.

Then came Dev, steady and quiet.

Dev: "I feel stuck, Guruji. No matter what I start, I don't finish. Opportunities come, but slip through. What is blocking me?"

Guruji's expression deepened.

"Ah. This is the subtle hand of a weakened Mercury—the planet of communication, coordination, and continuity. Your thoughts race ahead of your actions. Your mind writes stories your hands haven't yet caught up to. Strengthen Mercury, and you will find rhythm again."

He offered simple remedies:

"Wear green, especially on Wednesdays. Chant the Budh mantra daily. Hold an emerald, if it suits your chart. But above all—finish one thing before you begin another. Mercury rewards consistency, not cleverness alone."

Dev nodded slowly, as if some unseen knot had just loosened in his chest.

The Sacred Stillness Returns

Guruji looked around. The room was filled not with awe, but with intimacy. These were not teachings thrown from a mountaintop—they were like cups of warm water handed to the thirsty, each one personal, each one precise.

"Remember," he said softly, "the planets do not rule you. They only remind you. Of the energy you were born with, and the path you must walk to return to balance."

The devotees sat quietly, the weight of the world now strangely lighter. Not because it had disappeared—but because it had been understood.

The stars above were no longer distant. They were mirrors.

And through Guruji's voice, the cosmos had spoken in a language their hearts could finally hear.

The Brew of Inner Fire

The crisp morning light filtered through the swaying peepal leaves as the session in the Buddha Hall paused. With a soft smile that held both serenity and intent, he said,

"Let us now take a short break. Let the mind breathe. Let the heart steep in stillness—like tea that must be allowed to infuse."

The devotees slowly stood, their movements quiet and reverent. Outside the hall, the breeze carried the warm, earthy aroma of freshly brewed filter coffee and herbal infusions—tulsi, lemongrass, ginger. Cups clinked softly, and murmurs of reflection hovered like morning mist.

Apeksha, with her usual calm energy and storytelling spark, sat on the stone bench under the neem tree, her copper cup in hand. A few seekers gathered around instinctively—drawn to her like moths to a gentle flame. Kiran sipped his herbal tea, eyes half-closed, enjoying the quiet before the next plunge into cosmic inquiry.

Astyn asked her, "Apeksha, do you have a story for this still morning?"

She smiled knowingly, as though she had been waiting for the question all along.

"Yes," she said, "This one is about a blacksmith, a bell, and time…"

The Blacksmith's Bell: A Story of Inner Tempering

Long ago, in a small Himalayan village cloaked in snow, lived a blacksmith named Dheer. He was known not for his strength, but for his stillness—his ability to sit with metal as though it were a living soul.

He had been tasked by the temple elders to forge a great bell, one that would call the valley to prayer for generations. Every day, he worked beside the fire, melting and shaping the bronze with patience. But weeks passed. Months passed. Still, the bell remained unfinished.

The villagers began to question him. "Why does it take so long?" they asked. "Others would have made ten bells by now!"

Dheer said nothing.

What they didn't see was this: Every day, Dheer would hold the half-formed bell in the cold light of morning. He would strike it once and listen. Not to the sound it made—but to the silence that followed.

He was waiting for the moment when the silence after the strike would hum—not just in the air, but in his chest.

Then, one spring morning, he struck the bell—and he wept. Not from pain or exhaustion, but from knowing:

The bell had been tempered not just in fire, but in presence. It would now call the village—not just to prayer, but to presence itself.

The seekers sat in a still hush. A bird called from the guava tree overhead, and the breeze rustled through the teacups and shawls.

Apeksha concluded:

"Like Dheer, sometimes we must sit with our own fire longer than others understand. The world may rush us to produce, to act, to ring out before we're ready. But the soul... the soul waits for the moment when its silence sings back to it."

Kiran let out a soft sigh—deep, like a mountain exhale.

"That was beautiful," he whispered. "Let's see what Guruji has for us next."

And just then, as if cued by the very breath of the cosmos, the bell from the Buddha Hall rang gently—once, deep and mellow.

The devotees began to rise, holding their cups close, as though not wanting to spill even a drop of the wisdom that morning had offered.

CHAPTER VII

The Language of Light

The Language of Light — Understanding Planetary Strength

As the devotees returned to the Buddha Hall after the morning break, there was a soft silence, like the earth itself was inhaling wisdom.

The morning sun streamed into the Buddha Hall, each ray like a thread of gold weaving through the stillness. Silence blanketed the space, yet there was an electric anticipation in the air—a quiet reverence as the seekers awaited the day's unfolding wisdom.

Akshaya, a thoughtful and sincere young man, leaned forward slightly and asked with humility, "Guruji, what is the best way to assess the strength of the planets in a chart?"

Guruji nodded gently and replied with a smile that carried both patience and eternity.

"Akshaya, to assess the strength of the planets is to listen to how clearly the soul's instruments are tuned. Some notes are sharp, some are faint, and some are waiting to be played with the right hands."

He turned his gaze eastward, where the sun now lit the stone floor with an amber warmth.

"Let me offer you a story," he said.

The Potter and the Clay

"Once, in the valleys beneath the snowy veil of the Himalayas, lived a potter who worked with seven kinds of clay—each one unique, just like the planets. When the potter used each clay in its natural environment—with the right fire, air, and water—the pots emerged whole, strong, and beautiful. But when he tried to force clay into unfamiliar conditions, it cracked, lost its glow, or simply refused to take shape. He learned that the art was not just in shaping—but in respecting each clay's essence and origin."

Guruji turned back to Akshaya.

"This is how we must understand planetary strength. Not just in isolation—but in context, alignment, and resonance."

1. Own House: The Planet at Home

"When a planet is in its own house, it is like a king in his own palace—commanding, secure, and undisturbed. Mars in Aries or Scorpio acts decisively, instinctively, like a seasoned warrior on familiar terrain. Venus in Taurus or Libra brings beauty and balance with effortless grace. In these placements, the planet declares: 'Here, I know myself. I act without hesitation.'"

Guruji reached for a small sculpture of a lotus.

"As this lotus rests gently on water—its natural element—so does a planet bloom best in its native domain."

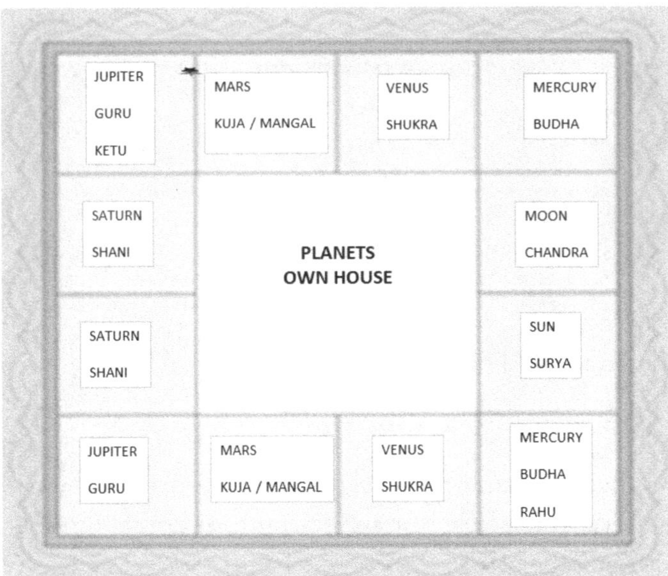

Illustration Own1: Planets in their own house.

2. Moolatrikona: The Planet in Its Sacred Temple

"Moolatrikona," Guruji explained, "is even more refined—it is not just the home, but the sacred sanctum of expression. For example, Jupiter in Sagittarius or Mercury in Virgo doesn't merely function—it teaches, guides, and inspires. These signs are the planet's workshop, its ashram, its sacred theatre."

He turned to Akshaya.

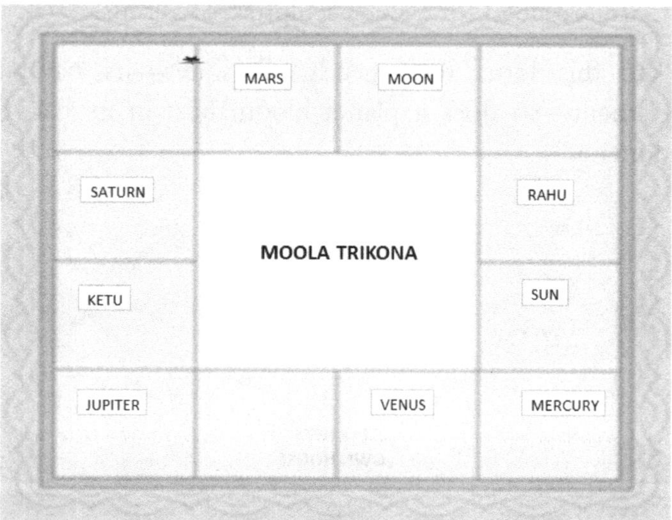

Illustration MT1: Moolatrikona.

"When a planet is in its moolatrikona sign, it is in service to dharma, not just strength. It uplifts the soul, not just the self."

3. Exaltation: The Planet at its Zenith

"Exaltation is when a planet reaches the peak of its potential, much like a flame burning in still air. The Moon in Taurus, for instance, gains emotional steadiness, nurturing from a place of grounded love. It is like a raga played in the perfect key, resonating through the heart with crystal clarity."

Guruji lifted his hand, palm open to the sun.

"Exaltation is not arrogance—it is harmony between the self and the universal intention. A planet here does not scream its truth—it sings it effortlessly."

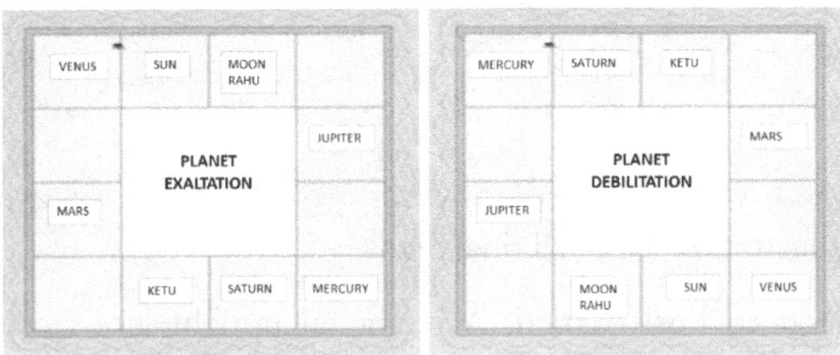

Illustration ED1: Exaltation and Deblitation.

4. Trinal Signs: The Sacred Geometry of Support

"The 1st, 5th, and 9th houses—these are trinal houses, sacred triangles of dharma and grace. Planets placed here are naturally supported, like a seed planted in fertile soil, or a traveller guided by favourable winds. They act not with strain, but with spontaneous alignment."

He turned again to Akshaya, whose face was now lit not just by the sun—but by insight.

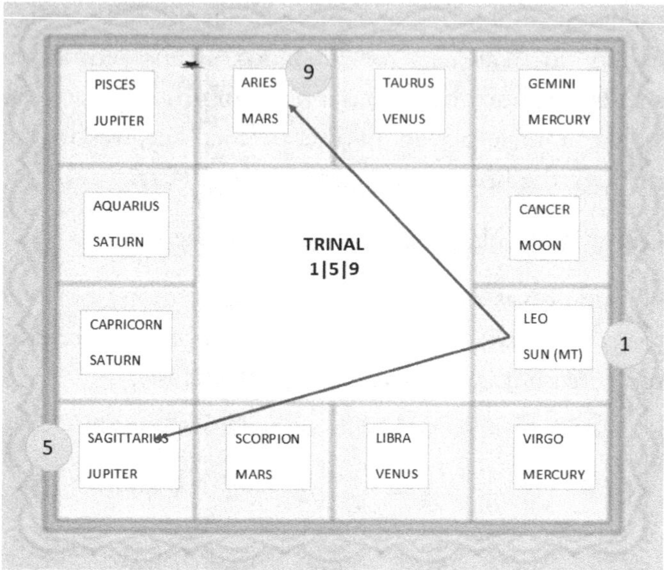

Illustration Trinal: Trinal Signs.

A deep hush settled. Akshaya sat upright, not from pride but presence. He could now see his own chart not as symbols on parchment, but as a map of light and intention. He saw the strong planets as pillars of purpose, and the weak ones as teachers in disguise, waiting for awareness to awaken them.

"So Guruji," he said softly, "a chart is not a sentence… but a language. A way the soul speaks through the planets?"

Guruji placed a gentle hand on his shoulder.

"Yes, Akshaya. The birth chart is a mantra—a vibration etched in time. And when you understand which planets are singing clearly, and which are waiting to be tuned by your awareness, you are no longer a seeker only… You become the conductor of your inner symphony."

CHAPTER VIII

Shadows of the Sky

The Music of the Planets – When Strength Hides in Silence

Guruji, with his voice low and steady, he said:

"Let us delve deeper into the understanding of planetary strength and weakness. For not all stars burn equally bright in every birth chart.

Some stumble. Some tremble.

But it is in their apparent weakness that we are offered a path—a sacred opportunity to rise."

He paused again and looked slowly around the hall, eyes meeting each devotee.

The Story of the Silent Musician

"There once was a boy," Guruji began, "named **Neel**, who lived in a village nestled in the shadow of the

Himalayas. Neel was born with a gift—the sitar sang through him.

His melodies carried the ache of the mountains and the whisper of the river. Villagers said even the wind slowed down to listen.

But fate can be a fierce teacher.

One winter, Neel lost the use of his right hand in an accident. His music came to an abrupt silence. The villagers mourned more than he did. 'A waste of talent,' they whispered.

But Neel… didn't stop.

He began to listen. To birds. To wind. To the soft pain that echoed in his own soul.

And then, slowly, he began to compose music in silence—through breath, rhythm, and thought.

He taught children to feel music before they played it. He taught widows to weep into the strings, not away from them.

And one day, a mystic visiting the village said,

'Neel no longer plays music.

Neel has become music.'

Guruji looked up, his eyes gleaming like the morning dew catching sunlight.

"This is how we must approach a debilitated planet in our chart—not as a failure, but as a redefinition of power.

When a planet can no longer shine in its usual brilliance, it invites us to seek depth instead of display, essence instead of expression."

Padma's Question: When Are Planets Weak?

Padma, seated near the central pillar, folded her hands and asked gently,

"Guruji, when exactly is a planet considered weak?"

Guruji nodded with warmth.

"Ah, Padma, just as a seed may struggle in rocky soil, so too can planets find themselves in conditions where their gifts struggle to emerge. Let me share with you the primary ways in which a planet may become 'weak'—or rather, challenged."

1. Debilitation – The Stray Note in a Foreign Scale

"A planet is **debilitated** when it is in a zodiac sign that opposes its natural essence.

Imagine a warrior (Mars) told to swim, or a poet (Venus) placed on a battlefield. Their **core nature** feels out of place.

- **Sun** in Libra – The sovereign struggles to find his throne.

- **Moon** in Scorpio – The mother drowns in hidden emotions.
- **Mars** in Cancer – The warrior becomes a wounded protector.

But remember: even in this tension, there is transformation. Like coal under pressure becomes diamond."

2. Combustion – Too Close to the Flame

"When a planet is too close to the Sun, it becomes combust—like a traveller who flies too near a torch and is scorched by the light.

- Mercury too close to the Sun may blur thoughts.
- Venus combust may bring confusion in love.

But again—where there is fire, there is purification.

A combust planet may lose its voice, but gain **clarity** in the long silence that follows."

3. Malefic Aspect – The Shadow on the Wall

"Just as even a bright lamp casts a shadow, so too can the aspect of malefic planets weaken or distort the gifts of another.

A benefic Moon might become anxious under Saturn's gaze.

A vibrant Mars might become reckless under Rahu's trickery.

But a shadow, dear ones, does not destroy the flame. It sharpens it. It teaches the soul to distinguish between true light and illusion."

4. Misaligned Tattwa – The Elemental Crosswind

"Every planet is born of a certain **element**—a tattwa. When placed in an opposing element, it behaves like fire underwater, or wind in a desert cave.

- **Mars** (fire) in **Cancer** (water): rage becomes repression.
- **Mercury** (air) in **Pisces** (water): logic becomes dreamy, scattered.

This is not a failure—it is a spiritual experiment.

To master a planet in an incompatible element is to alchemise fire and water—to make steam and rise."

Transmutation Over Correction

Guruji after a pause said:

"Your weak planets are not curses.

They are invitations—to deeper power, subtler insight, greater grace.

A weak voice may one day become the most powerful silence.

So don't rush to fix.

First… **listen.**

Then… **transform.**"

The hall was silent, like a temple deep beneath the sea.

Some devotees had tears in their eyes—not from sorrow, but from relief. They were no longer broken. They were being **reshaped**.

When Planets Whisper – The Path of Remedies

Kiran, softly asked, "Guruji… if the planets are weakened, how can we strengthen them?"

Guruji smiled, and with a tone both tender and luminous, replied:

"A weak planet is like a child who's lost in a crowd—not gone, not broken, just waiting to be called back home.
And the way we call them… is through remedy. But not all remedies are the same. Some require action, some surrender. Some require voice, others silence."

Sun – The Father, Ego, Authority

Weak Sun leads to a lack of confidence, fear of authority, and weak willpower.

Remedies:

Mantra: "ॐ घृणि सूर्याय नमः" (Om Ghrini Suryaya Namah) – chant at sunrise.

Beej Mantra: "ॐ ह्रां ह्रीं ह्रौं सः सूर्याय नमः" (**Om Hraam Hreem Hraum Sah Suryay Namah**)

Charity: Offer red cloth, wheat, or copper on Sundays.

Spiritual Practice: Surya Namaskar (Sun Salutation), early rising.

Gemstone: Ruby set in gold on right-hand ring finger (if astrologically suitable).

"The Sun is your inner throne. When dimmed, serve the kingdom with humility, and the king within shall rise again."

Moon – The Mother, Mind, Emotions

A weak Moon brings emotional instability, anxiety, lack of peace.

Remedies:

Mantra: "ॐ चन्द्राय नमः" (Om Chandraya Namah)

Beej Mantra: "ॐ श्रां श्रीं श्रौं सः चंद्रमसे नमः" (**Om Shraam Shreem Shraum Sah Chandramase Namah**)

Charity: Offer white rice, milk, or silver to women or temples on Mondays.

Spiritual Practice: Spend time near water, moon-gazing, journaling.

Gemstone: Pearl in silver on the little finger (right hand).

"The Moon doesn't roar—it reflects. To strengthen it, still the waters of your heart, and you shall see the stars in your soul."

Mars – The Warrior, Drive, Courage

A weak Mars may cause laziness, anger, or physical weakness.

Remedies:

Mantra: "ॐ भौमाय नमः" (Om Bhaumaya Namah)

Beeja Mantra: "ॐ क्रां क्रीं क्रौं सः भौमाय नमः" (Om Kram Kreem Kraum Sah Bhaumaya Namah)

Charity: Donate red lentils or jaggery on Tuesdays.

Spiritual Practice: Physical discipline (martial arts, yoga), helping siblings.

Gemstone: Red Coral in copper on the ring finger.

"Mars is fire. If it falters, become the hearth—contain the flame and let it warm, not burn."

Mercury – The Messenger, Intellect, Communication

Weak Mercury causes confusion, nervous speech, and poor memory.

Remedies:

Mantra: "ॐ बुधाय नमः" (Om Budhaya Namah)

Beej Mantra: "ॐ ब्रां ब्रीं ब्रौं सः बुधाय नमः" (**Om Braam Breem Braum Sah Budhay Namah**)

Charity: Green clothes, moong dal (green gram), or books on Wednesdays.

Spiritual Practice: Writing, public speaking, or serving the young and intelligent.

Gemstone: Emerald in gold or silver.

"Mercury is your inner flute—if silent, cleanse your breath and your words. Wisdom will play its song again."

Jupiter – The Guru, Wisdom, Dharma

Weak Jupiter leads to a lack of direction, poor judgment, or loss of faith.

Remedies:

Mantra: "ॐ गुरवे नमः" or **"ॐ बृं बृहस्पतये नमः"** (**Om Gurave Namah**)

Beej Mantra: "ॐ ग्रां ग्रीं ग्रौं सः गुरुवे नमः" (**Om Gram Greem Graum Sah Gurave Namah**)

Charity: Donate yellow sweets, books, turmeric on Thursdays.

Spiritual Practice: Seek a guru, teach, follow dharma, and perform acts of generosity.

Gemstone: Yellow Sapphire in gold on the index finger.

"Jupiter is not just a planet—it is your conscience. To awaken it, **walk your talk**, and walk in grace."

Venus – Love, Art, Relationships

Weak Venus brings disharmony, loneliness, or sensory imbalance.

Remedies:

Mantra: "ॐ शुक्राय नमः" (Om Shukraya Namah)

Beej Mantra: "ॐ शां शीं शूं सः शुक्राय नमः" (**Om Shum Shum Shaum Sah Shukraya Namaha**)

Charity: White clothes, sweets, ghee, to women or artists on Fridays.

Spiritual Practice: Music, dance, appreciation of beauty, devotion to Lakshmi.

Gemstone: Diamond or **White Sapphire**.

"Venus is the fragrance of a rose unseen. If dim, learn again to love yourself like a poet adores silence."

Saturn – Karma, Discipline, Detachment

Weak Saturn may cause delays, fear, burdens, or a poverty mindset.

Remedies:

Mantra: "ॐ शं शनैश्चराय नमः" (Om Sham Shanaishcharaya Namah)

Beej mantra: "ॐ शां शीं शूं सः शनैश्चराय नमः" (Om Praam Preem Praum Sah Shanaishcharaaya Namah)

Charity: Black sesame, mustard oil, footwear, to the poor or elderly on Saturdays.

Spiritual Practice: Service to the downtrodden, silent work, meditation.

Gemstone: Blue Sapphire (with utmost care and only under guidance).

"Saturn does not deny. It delays so you may become **worthy**. Serve, endure, and bloom in your own time."

Rahu – The Seeker, Obsession, Shadow

Imbalanced Rahu creates illusions, addictions, or restless ambition.

Remedies:

Mantra: "ॐ राहवे नमः" (Om Rahave Namah)

Beej Mantra: "ॐ भ्रां भ्रीं भ्रौं सः राहवे नमः" (Om Bhraam Bhreem Bhraum Saha Rahave Namah)

Charity: Mustard oil, blankets, and black urad dal on Saturdays.

Spiritual Practice: Shadow work, fasting, silence, confronting inner fears.

"Rahu is the smoke that teaches you to seek the flame. Do not fear it—**understand it**."

Ketu – The Mystic, Detachment, Past Karma

Imbalanced Ketu causes isolation, confusion, or spiritual disconnection.

Remedies:

Mantra: "ॐ केतवे नमः" (Om Ketave Namah)

Beej Mantra: "ॐ स्रां स्रीं स्रौं सः केतवे नमः" (Om Sraam Sreem Sraum Sah Ketave Namah)

Charity: Brown items, sesame seeds, feeding stray dogs.

Spiritual Practice: Surrender, moksha-oriented practices, ancestral healing.

"Ketu is the falling leaf—it does not resist. It teaches you that liberation comes not by holding on, but by letting go."

Guruji softly said:

"Remedies are not rituals alone—they are relationships. Between you and the cosmos. Between you and the self you're still discovering. When the stars within you realign, the stars above you follow."

The Fire Beneath the Ash – A Story from Apeksha's Past

The breeze rustled gently through the leaves of the ancient Banyan tree, its branches stretched wide like the open arms of a wise sage. Afternoon light filtered down in golden threads, dancing on the earth like blessings too subtle to speak aloud.

The devotees had gathered after lunch—Abhilasha, Akanksh, Akshatha, Roopa, Bhavya, Aarna, Dev, and John. The group had settled into a calm hush, sipping warm herbal tea, when Lalitha turned to Apeksha, her voice soft but expectant.

"Apeksha, will you share an incident from one of your past retreats?"

There was a moment's stillness.

Apeksha, who had been watching the play of sunlight on the earth, nodded slowly. Her eyes softened. She placed her cup down and leaned forward.

"Yes," she said. "I will tell you about the year I lost my way—and found my silence."

The Story: The Fire Beneath the Ash

"It was a retreat much like this one," Apeksha began, "in the hills of Chikmagalur, where mist cloaks the trees like sacred breath. I had been restless. I had come not to seek peace, but to demand answers. I was undergoing difficult times. My identity had burned, but the ashes clung."

"On the third day, the Guru at that retreat announced: 'Today, you will spend the whole day in silence. No books. No writing. No mantra. Just observe.'"

Some devotees shifted. Silence can be harder than noise.

"At first, I wandered. I watched ants. I stared at the clouds. I grew impatient. Angry. But by midday, I sat beneath a tree much like this one and began to cry—not out of sorrow, but exhaustion. I realised I wasn't grieving the end of things, but the absence of distraction. All my life, I had poured my pain into motion: into people, work, music, travel. But now there was nowhere to run. Just the silence. And me."

Apeksha's voice grew steadier.

"In that moment, I heard something. Not outside, but within. A soft whisper—not words, just presence. Like someone had placed a hand on my heart and said, 'You're still here. Beneath all of it—you're still here.'"

She looked at the others now, eyes misty but radiant.

"From that day, my practice changed. I stopped praying for signs and started listening for silence. I stopped chasing fire and started tending the glow beneath the ash."

Reflections Under the Banyan Tree

There was a long, sacred pause.

Even the wind seemed to hush, as if the Banyan tree itself was absorbing the story—adding it to the rings of wisdom hidden in its great trunk.

Roopa wiped a quiet tear. Dev looked down, thoughtful. Akshatha had her hands clasped, as if holding something fragile and precious.

Finally, Kiran exhaled.

"It's going to be a long path," he said. "But maybe… that's the point."

The others nodded.

Just then, the bell sounded from the Buddha Hall, calling them back for the next session.

They rose slowly, not wanting to break the circle too quickly. As they walked, the earth felt softer, the wind gentler, and the inner space—wider.

CHAPTER IX

The Dance of Shadows

The Dance of Shadows – When Rahu and Ketu Obstruct the Light

The morning session had ended, but a strange heaviness lingered in the air, like the scent of unspoken truths.

After the lunch break, the devotees gathered again. A soft breeze passed through the open windows of the Buddha Hall. A bird called in the distance, its cry echoing like a forgotten memory.

Guruji entered slowly, his steps deliberate, as though walking through time itself. The devotees sat straighter.

He looked at them with a gentle yet piercing gaze and said:

"Today we speak of shadows—not to fear them, but to understand their shape."

There was a long silence, the kind that feels like listening with the soul.

The Story of the Mirror Without a Face

Guruji began:

"In a quiet village at the edge of the Vindhyas, there lived a sculptor named Aditya. Known for his lifelike statues, people came from distant lands to commission his work. But there was one sculpture he could never finish—a mirror without a face.

'I see everyone else so clearly,' he would say, 'but when I sculpt myself, I lose the image before it's done. It disappears.'

What he didn't know was this: the mirror he was crafting was watched over by two unseen guardians—Rahu and Ketu, the shadow planets. They veiled his vision not out of malice, but so he would first find the truth within, before trying to reflect it outside."

Guruji turned toward the devotees.

"Rahu and Ketu are not enemies. They are guardians of karmic thresholds. They test us by veiling clarity, by bending reality—so we may learn to trust the eye within, not just the eyes we see with."

When Rahu or Ketu Block the Light

Guruji moved closer to the whiteboard and gently wrote the names Rahu and Ketu.

"They do not have bodies, yet they control so much. They are like smoke: you can't grasp it, but it blurs your vision. When Rahu or Ketu conjoin or aspect other planets, their influence can cause confusion, delay, and distortion.

They may cloud Jupiter's wisdom, disturb the Moon's peace, or twist Mercury's logic. The impact? A brilliant speaker forgets their words. A wise man questions his own judgment. A mother feels a sudden distance from her child.

But remember…"

Guruji paused, his eyes shining softly.

"What Rahu and Ketu obscure, they also compel us to master. They are the mist we must learn to walk through."

Remedies for Rahu and Ketu

Guruji continued:

1. Mantra & Ritual:

"Chanting mantras like 'Om Raam Rahave Namah' and 'Om Ketave Namah' is not just repetition. It is tuning your vibration to see through illusion. It is blowing gently on the mirror until the fog clears."

2. Gemstones:

"Gemstones such as Hessonite (Gomed) for Rahu and Cat's Eye (Lehsunia) for Ketu can stabilise their influence. But only under strict guidance. These are not ornaments—they are instruments."

3. Spiritual Practice:

"Engage in meditation, especially on shadow work—facing hidden fears, past traumas, karmic loops. When the mind stops resisting, Rahu bows. When the ego lets go, Ketu dissolves."

When Planets Are Obstructed by Malefics

Padma leaned forward. "And what about Saturn or Mars? They, too, can block other planets…"

Guruji nodded slowly.

"Yes. Malefics like Saturn, Mars, Rahu, Ketu—they do not destroy light, but test its strength. A malefic aspect is like a mountain placed before a flowing river. It doesn't stop the water—it simply teaches it to carve new paths."

To identify obstruction:

Look at the aspected planet. What house is it in? What role does it play?

Study the malefic's nature. Is it discipline (Saturn), aggression (Mars), or illusion (Rahu)?

To resolve the obstruction:

Chant the obstructed planet's mantra. Not to dominate, but to invite it to speak again.

Offer what it loves. Jupiter loves teaching. Venus adores beauty. Feed the planet with your behaviour.

Balance the tattwa (element). If a fiery Mars is harming a watery Moon, introduce cooling rituals—like moon baths, milk offerings, or peaceful fasting.

When Planets Are Simply Weak

Kiran, quiet until now, asked, "And Guruji, when planets are not blocked—but simply... tired?"

Guruji smiled, as though he had waited for this moment.

"Ah, Kiran… A weak planet is like a tired child. It has not been punished, it has just been ignored. Such planets long for attention, respect, and harmony."

Strengthen them through:

Gemstones (with caution and guidance).

Mantras (spoken with devotion, not mechanical recitation).

Charity and acts of seva. For example, is Saturn weak? Serve the elderly. Mercury weak? Donate books or teach children.

"Remember—no planet is truly weak if your intent is strong."

The air had grown thick with silence and understanding. The shadows of the Hall danced gently as the afternoon sun lowered.

“When a planet is blocked or weakened, do not seek control—seek communion. The sky is not against you. Sometimes, it only clouds your path so you may learn to walk by inner stars.”

CHAPTER X

Yantras

Vasudeva Asked, "Guruji, What is a Yantra?" A Discourse in the Buddha Hall

The evening breeze danced through the lattice of the Buddha Hall, gently rustling the prayer flags. The oil lamps flickered like the breath of the Divine.

Vasudeva, seated among the devotees, asked with folded hands, "Guruji, what is a Yantra?"

A hush fell.

Guruji smiled, as if unwrapping an invisible secret.

"Yantra," he said softly, "means machine… but not in the way you think. It is a mystical diagram, a living geometry, carved not just on copper or stone, but etched into the sacred fabric of the universe."

He paused, letting the silence deepen.

"Imagine the Divine as a vast ocean of energy—boundless, formless, silent. Now imagine taking a copper bowl and drawing a circle, a triangle, a dot… That diagram is a Yantra—a portal. A way to bring that infinite energy into form, into purpose, into relationship."

Some devotees closed their eyes, feeling the pulse of what was being spoken.

"A Yantra is the stillness in motion, the wheel that turns while remaining unmoved." Guruji looked at Vasudeva. "It is not merely an object—it is a sadhana, a journey."

He turned to the gathering and continued.

"A Yantra may be used to meditate upon a deity, yes. Or to unlock an inner strength. Or to protect one's home, attract abundance, or heal the body. But these are only the outer uses. Its real power lies in aligning your soul with the cosmos—like tuning an instrument to the eternal raga of creation."

Then, Guruji leaned forward, eyes glowing like the morning sun breaking through clouds.

"Let me tell you a story," he said.

The Cursed Blessing of the Navagrahas

"In ancient times," Guruji began, "there lived a noble sage named Kalava. Afflicted with leprosy and many other terrible diseases, he could no longer walk to temples. So he simply sat beneath a tree and sang the names of the Navagrahas—the nine planetary gods—his voice full of pain and devotion."

"He offered no rituals. No gold. No incense. Just surrender."

The devotees listened in silence, the only sound the soft call of a koel in the trees outside.

"The planets were moved. They descended to Earth and healed him. Kalava wept in gratitude. But in the heavens, Brahma, the god of creation, was furious. 'How can the planets grant boons?' he thundered. 'That is not their dharma!' In his rage, he cursed the Navagrahas with leprosy and banished them to a desolate forest called Vellurukku Vanam—the forest of white wildflowers."

"The Navagrahas, once resplendent celestial forces, now diseased and cast down, wandered in anguish."

"But all is not lost," Guruji whispered.

"They turned their eyes to Lord Shiva, the One who sees what others refuse to see. Shiva, ever compassionate, appeared before them and said, 'This land shall be yours now. From this place, you will bless the devotees who come to you. Your curse shall become your altar.'"

Guruji closed his eyes briefly. "This is the secret of the Yantra."

"It is not born from perfection. It is born from fall and redemption, from curse turned into blessing, from chaos given sacred form."

He looked around the Buddha Hall, "The Yantra is your own life—when you dare to bring stillness to your chaos, symmetry to your sorrow, discipline to your longing."

A tear fell down a devotee's cheek.

Another softly recited, "Om Namah Sivaya."

Guruji concluded:

"Yantras are not drawn. They are received—through surrender, patience, and the silence of grace. Worship them, yes. But more than that, become them. Let every part of your being—your thoughts, your actions, your silence—become a sacred design through which the Divine may descend."

And in the golden hush of the Buddha Hall, even the air seemed to hold its breath, as if the Yantra of the universe had just turned one more perfect rotation.

Vasudeva asked, bowing, "Guruji… we have heard of the planets—the Navagrahas—who govern our karma. But you once said that they even respond to Yantras. What are these Yantras, and how do they work for each graha?"

Guruji opened his eyes, slow as a sunrise.

"They are not drawings," he said softly. "They are conversations... between your soul and the cosmic forces that shape your journey."

1. Surya Yantra – The Mirror of Truth

"Surya, the Sun, is your core, your Atma Shakti. His Yantra is radiant, geometric fire—concentric triangles pointing outward, symbolising light breaking through shadow."

Use: When you lack clarity, self-confidence, or purpose. When father issues, health, or leadership are karmic themes.

Meditate with it to awaken your dignity, your right to shine.

"It does not inflate your ego," Guruji said. "It humbles you to the truth."

2. Chandra Yantra – The Vessel of Feeling

"Moon's Yantra is soft, circular, curved—like ripples in a still pond. It calms the churning mind."

Use: For mental peace, emotional healing, fertility, and mother karma.

"This Yantra," Guruji whispered, "teaches you to hold sorrow without drowning in it. It is a bowl that catches even your tears and turns them into pearls."

3. Mangal Yantra – The Flame of Will

"Mars is the fire of action, the architect of courage. His Yantra is sharp—interlocking triangles, masculine, assertive."

Use: In litigation, when fighting for justice, or healing anger and impulsiveness. For blood-related issues and property disputes.

"It is not about aggression," Guruji said. "It teaches you sacred warfare—the war within."

4. Budha Yantra – The Dance of Mind

"Mercury's Yantra is intelligent, clean, precise—a woven geometry of circles and squares."

Use: For speech, education, communication, business, and writing. Especially helpful for students, writers, and negotiators.

"Budha's Yantra teaches how to think without being trapped in thought," Guruji said. "It teaches the sword and the song."

5. Guru Yantra – The Staircase to Heaven

"Jupiter, the Guru, the Guide. His Yantra is expansive, golden, and full of benevolent balance."

Use: To enhance spiritual growth, education, wealth, and grace. Also for overcoming curses and expanding one's dharma.

"This Yantra," Guruji said, "does not give you answers. It makes you worthy of answers. It turns the student into a teacher."

6. Shukra Yantra – The Rose of Union

"Venus is the lover, the artist, the harmoniser. His Yantra is symmetrical, soothing, a garden of forms."

Use: For marriage, relationships, art, prosperity, beauty, and reproductive healing.

"It whispers," Guruji said gently, "Can you love without possession? Can you create without ego? Shukra's Yantra is not for pleasure—it is for devotion disguised as delight."

7. Shani Yantra – The Geometry of Time

"Saturn is the slow grind, the architect of patience. His Yantra is angular, disciplined, square-based."

Use: In times of long karma, financial delays, depression, and existential crises.

"This Yantra is not easy," Guruji said. "It's a mirror that shows you the chains you built… and the key hidden inside them."

8. Rahu Yantra – The Smoke of Desire

"Rahu is the head without the body, the unquenchable thirst. His Yantra is hypnotic, disorienting—fractals without centre."

Use: For dealing with obsession, illusion, sudden gains or losses, foreign travel, and breaking ancestral patterns.

"Rahu's Yantra," Guruji said, "is a maze—but not to trap you. To teach you that even illusion is part of the awakening."

9. Ketu Yantra – The Liberation Blade

"Ketu is the body without the head. Moksha Karaka—the giver of release. His Yantra is inward—subtle, dissolving, serpent-like."

Use: For spiritual detachment, breaking past-life karmas, psychic abilities, and deep meditation.

"It unknots the knots," said Guruji. "Ketu's Yantra is not for seekers of success. It is for those ready to vanish into the One."

"Yantras," Guruji said, "are not superstition. They are soul science. But don't approach them like shortcuts. Approach them like prayers."

He looked at the disciples.

"Don't just place a Yantra in your home. Place it in your awareness. Breathe it. Live it. Let it rewire your destiny—not through force, but through alignment."

And in the stillness that followed, the Yantras did not feel like diagrams anymore.

They felt like doorways.

Surya Yantra – The Radiant Mind

6	7	2
1	5	9
8	3	4

"Surya's yantra is a fire in stillness. This square aligns the seeker with clarity, courage, health, and the royal path of dharma. Place it in the East — the direction of sunrise — and it ignites the soul with purpose. This is not merely mathematics; this is the geometry of inner light."

Chandra Yantra – The Mirror of Still Waters

7	8	3
2	6	10
9	4	5

"Chandra's yantra calms the lunar tides of the mind. Its numbers weave a soft net of balance and receptivity. Ideal for those battling anxiety, insomnia, or emotional imbalance. The moon does not argue with the night — she simply reflects."

Mangal Yantra – The Blade of Will

8	9	4
3	7	11
10	5	6

"Mars governs drive, protection, and passion. His yantra strengthens bones, resolve, and boundaries. For warriors in the inner or outer world, this yantra is a sword resting in silence. Channel it not in haste — but in focused action."

Budha Yantra – The Grid of Wisdom

9	10	5
4	8	12
11	6	7

"Budha — the planet of intellect — rules wit, speech, and transactions. This yantra sharpens memory, heals misunderstandings, and reveals clarity in chaos. When used before study, exams, or negotiations, it tunes the tongue to truth."

Guru Yantra – The Tree of Benediction

10	11	6
5	9	3
12	7	8

"Jupiter is the preceptor of devas, the guardian of dharma. His yantra blesses with children, grace, expansion, and higher knowledge. This is the yantra of teachers, parents, priests, and those seeking light beyond logic. Meditate upon it with gratitude."

Shukra Yantra – The Lotus of Desire

11	12	7

6	10	14
13	8	9

"Shukra, planet of beauty and art, offers this yantra for attraction, romance, creativity, and wealth. It radiates magnetic charm. Place it near mirrors or musical instruments to amplify Venusian vibration. But remember — beauty without devotion becomes bondage."

Shani Yantra – The Stairway of Patience

12	13	8
7	11	5
14	9	10

"Saturn — the slow walker — tests the soul. His yantra offers discipline, longevity, justice, and liberation through labour. It is a silent staircase that leads to freedom — but only one step at a time. Honour it when life feels heavy, and you will find steel within."

Rahu Yantra – The Smoke Mirror

13	14	9
8	12	16
15	10	11

"Rahu's yantra is the talisman of transformation. It protects against deception, enhances foreign travels, breaks illusions, and opens hidden doors. But beware

— it is a wild tide. Anchor your intent before invoking his power."

Ketu Yantra – The Flame of Moksha

14	15	10
9	13	17
16	11	12

"Ketu dissolves identity. His yantra is for those who are ready to transcend. It heals ancestral karma, guides spiritual awakening, and unbinds the soul from worldly clutches. Place this yantra where you meditate or keep sacred ashes — it is the mark of the seer."

The Yantra is a Mirror of the Self

Guruji closed his eyes and said: "When you place these yantras on your altar, remember: they are not decorations. They are living diagrams — formulas in sacred code. Respect them. Feed them with mantras. Offer your silence. And over time… you will not just see their power. You will become it."

The golden sun had lowered itself into the arms of the horizon, painting the sky in shades of amber and lavender. The silence of the Buddha Hall gave way to the gentle murmur of rustling leaves and the clinking of coffee cups. The air was rich — not just with the aroma of fresh coffee — but with a sense of stillness, as if time itself had bowed down to listen.

The devotees gathered under the ancient banyan tree, whose roots hung like meditative monks suspended in surrender. Kiran, Sam, Alice, Sofia, Bhavya, Aarna, Dev, and John sat in a quiet circle. Soon, Akshaya, Padma, Vasudeva, Vidyarthi, Aastha, and Abhirami joined, their eyes gleaming from the discourse they had just absorbed.

Apeksha moved among them with a soft smile, passing warm cups of coffee, her presence as comforting as the drink itself.

Then, in the golden hush, Nita leaned forward and said,

"Apeksha… why don't you share something? A story. Something from your heart."

Kieron chuckled and teased,

"Yes, come on Apeksha. We've seen your silence… let us hear your voice tonight."

Apeksha hesitated — her fingers tightening slightly around the coffee pot. But then, a soft wind kissed her cheek, and she looked up at the great banyan. Perhaps she heard Guruji's words echoing faintly in her mind.

She sat down, folded her legs gently, and began, her voice like river water — slow, clear, flowing.

The Lamp That Waited

"There was once a small village nestled between forest and river, where the nights were long, and electricity had never touched its soil. In one of the oldest houses of the village lived a grandmother named Amba.

Every evening, as dusk began to settle, she would light a single clay lamp — her only source of light. She called it 'Deepa', and she treated it like a companion.

She would whisper to it: 'You must stay awake when I grow tired.' 'You must remember what I forget.'"

The devotees listened, coffee forgotten.

"Now, Amba had a granddaughter, Meena, a city-born girl who visited only during vacations. One summer, when Meena was twelve, she came to stay for a few weeks. She was full of energy, dreams, and impatience. She found the village too quiet, the people too slow, and that old lamp — laughable.

'Why don't you get a torch, Dadi(Grandmother)? Or at least a candle?' she asked.

Amba just smiled and said, 'Some lights show you the world… and some remind you of the world inside you.'"

Apeksha's voice began to tremble slightly — but it wasn't weakness. It was the emotion of presence.

"One stormy night, the village plunged into deeper darkness. The skies roared, and the river rose. Meena was scared. The window flapped open, and the wind howled like an animal.

She ran to Amba's room.

But Amba wasn't there.

Only the little clay lamp was burning — steady, strong, as if saying, 'Wait.' Meena, shivering, sat before it.

Minutes passed. Maybe hours. And in that time, something happened. The fear slowly began to dissolve — not because the storm stopped, but because the light never did.

Meena stared at that flame until she felt a silence inside her. And when Amba returned from helping a neighbour, she found Meena asleep… peaceful… beside the lamp."

Apeksha looked at everyone, her eyes a little moist, her voice like the edge of a whisper now.

"Years later, when Amba passed, Meena returned as a grown woman. She lit the same lamp again in the house. And now, whenever life storms inside her — she sits before a small clay flame in her apartment in Mumbai… and remembers."

She looked at Nita and smiled.

"So you see, Nita… some stories don't have big endings. But they leave a small flame inside you, that never goes out."

Silence.

Even the banyan leaves stood still, listening.

Then Sofia whispered,

"Was that your story, Apeksha?"

Apeksha just smiled and turned away, sipping her coffee.

And that night, something had changed under the banyan tree — not in the stars above, but in the hearts gathered below.

CHAPTER XI

Temples

Guruji said, "In the grand cosmic dance of the Navagrahas — the nine celestial intelligences — there is one around whom all revolve. One who neither boasts nor retreats. One who simply is. That One... is Surya."

"He is the sovereign light, the divine witness, the source of all prana — life force. Therefore, in the sacred architecture of the temple, Surya is placed at the centre of the Navagraha mandala — the cosmic compass of the planets. Around him, the others take their place, not randomly, not aesthetically, but in divine precision."

"This centrality is not merely symbolic. It is existential. It is ontological. It reminds us: without inner Surya — the spiritual sun — all other energies scatter, confused and directionless. Surya is not just the king among planets. He is the throne on which all others are seated."

The Geometry of Grace – No Two Facing Each Other

Guruji gestured to a small wooden model before him — nine miniature murtis placed in a circular formation.

"No two grahas face each other."

"Because in the cosmic order, confrontation is chaos. Each energy must operate in harmony, not in a duel. The planets are not rivals. They are aspects of the One — and when placed correctly, they form the divine wheel of time, karma, and transformation."

"That is why these murtis are placed upon a pedestal, often three feet high — the height symbolising Triloka — the three realms of existence: Bhuloka (earth), Antariksha (sky), and Swarga (heaven). And this Navagraha Peetha is not placed casually — it resides to the northeast of the sanctum, the Ishanya corner, where the energy of divine blessings naturally flows."

The Nine Parikramas – Walking the Solar Spiral

"Worship of the Navagrahas is not a mere ritual. It is a return to inner orbit. A realignment. That is why devotees perform nine circumambulations (parikramas) around the deities — a clockwise spiral of surrender. With each turn, the soul unwinds its karma and steps deeper into resonance with cosmic rhythm."

"And with each round, a chant — a bija, a mantra, a vibration for each graha — must be offered. For each has a day. Each has a frequency. Each has a door through which we may enter the sanctum of our own destiny."

Two Patterns: Agama and Vaidika Pradishta – The Two Eyes of the Tradition

Vasudeva asked softly, "Guruji, why are there two different arrangements — Agama and Vaidika Pradishta? Which one is correct?"

Guruji smiled, as if the question itself was light.

"There is not one eye to see truth, child. There are two — Agama and Veda. Just like Shiva's eyes — one perceives the form, the other the formless. One sees the structured temple, the other the eternal temple within."

Agama Pradishta – Surya at the Core of the Web

"In the Agama Pradishta, Surya is placed at the centre like the axis of a chariot wheel. Around him, the other grahas are positioned:

- Chandra in the East (emotion aligning with dawn)
- Budha in the South (logic grounding action)
- Brihaspati in the West (wisdom anchoring sunset)
- Shukra in the North (love aspiring upward)

- Mangala in the South-East (energy emerging like flame)
- Shani in the South-West (karma weighing like stone)
- Rahu in the North-West (illusion whispering from the edge)
- Ketu in the North-East (moksha awaiting like mist)"

"This is followed in sacred shrines like Suryanar Kovil, Tiruvidaimarudur, and others — places where Surya reigns with unmistakable presence."

Vaidika Pradishta – The Vedic Compass of Forces

"In Vaidika Pradishta, Surya still reigns at the centre, but the surrounding order shifts like a different raga of the same truth:

- Shukra in the East
- Mangala in the South
- Shani in the West
- Brihaspati in the North
- Chandra in the South-East
- Rahu in the South-West
- Ketu in the North-West
- Budha in the North-East"

"This layout is more aligned with the Vedic mapping of energies based on elemental balance, ritual context, and metaphysical correspondences. It is not a contradiction — it is a complement. Like Shiva dancing as Bhairava in one temple, and as Ardhanarishvara in another."

A Story from the Forest of Light

Guruji leaned back, his eyes drifting toward a candle flame. Then, he began a story.

"In the forest of Aruna, a little boy named Pradyumna was born blind. Yet he had a radiant voice and sang the Vedas like he could see the stars themselves. One day, he asked the village priest, 'Can I see Surya?'

The priest, unsure how to answer, took him to an old Navagraha temple lost in vines. The boy placed his hand on the Sun murti and simply said, 'You are warm.' Then he walked nine times around the deities, whispering their names like old friends. At the end, he sat down… and wept.

'Why are you crying?' asked the priest.

'Because,' said the blind boy, 'I just saw the Sun. Not with these eyes… but with the one that was never blind.'_

That night, they say, a golden light burst from the Navagraha Peetha — and the boy was never seen again. Only his song echoes sometimes… when the wind passes through the temple trees."_

Guruji looked around at the gathered souls, now immersed in silence.

"Surya in the centre reminds us — life is not to be lived from the periphery, but from the core. And each graha — each planetary deity — is a ray of the One Light, teaching us the many colours of karma, time, and transcendence."

"Perform the nine parikramas not just with your feet… but with your life. Let your actions orbit the Divine. And you will find — like the blind boy in the forest — that the Sun has always been within you."

When the Cosmos Took Stone:

Guruji began, his voice flowing like a river through silence, "you think temples are built with stone and sweat… but they are not. They are built with insight. With vision. With the understanding that if God lives in the stars, then God must also sit in form — somewhere in the temple of the Earth."

"And so, the rishis carved the planets — not to worship them, but to walk through them. Each arrangement is not random. It is a map of consciousness."

He looked around slowly, as if letting the words find each devotee's heart.

1. Gangaikonda Cholapuram – The Solar Flower

"At Gangaikonda Cholapuram, the Nine Grahas are sculpted from a single stone. Surya, the sovereign, is at the centre — like the Sun in your solar plexus, the Manipura. Around him, eight deities whirl like petals, facing each cardinal direction."

Guruji pointed to a mandala in the air with his hand.

"This is not a stone carving. It is a living yantra — a spiritual solar system. Just as the grahas orbit the Sun, so must your karma revolve around your dharma.

You are the chariot, the body. The seven horses are your energy channels. The charioteer is your mind. And Surya… is your soul.

When that chariot faces truth, the wheel of life becomes your friend. When it turns away, it becomes your prison."

2. Suryanar Koil, Kumbakonam – The Silent Guru Behind the Horse

"In Suryanar Koil, each graha has a separate shrine — but Brihaspati, the planet of wisdom, is not given a shrine of his own.

Instead, he stands behind a horse statue, directly facing the Sun."

The disciples looked puzzled. Guruji smiled gently.

"It is to say — the true Guru never stands in front. He stands behind the chariot of your soul, guiding it silently, never asking for worship. The ego wants a shrine. But wisdom wants clarity."

3. Devipattinam – The Temple in the Sea

Guruji's tone turned reverent, his eyes misting.

"At Devipattinam, the Navagrahas are not inside a stone temple. They sit quietly inside the sea itself — as stones said to be consecrated by Lord Rama himself."

"Each of these stones," he whispered, "was formed from poisonous elements, carefully blended into an eternal medicine. That is your life too. Your past wounds, your regrets, your sorrows — alone, they are poison. But when digested with devotion, they become amrita — nectar.

That temple reminds us — some of our greatest blessings are buried in water, where only the brave can bow."

4. Vaitheswarankoil – The Line of Fate

"At Vaitheswarankoil, the Nine Grahas are aligned in a perfect straight line. Why?"

"Because sometimes, the universe says: Now walk straight. No curves, no comforts, no escape. Now you must walk through your karma, one step at a time."

"This temple is not just for worship. It is for those in hard Saturn periods, Rahu Mahadasha, or life's long nights. It teaches — order is grace. Even pain has precision."

5. Tanjore Brihadisvara – Nine Lingas, Not Planets

"At Tanjore, there are no statues of the Navagrahas. Instead, there are Navalingas — nine Shiva lingams, each representing a graha."

Guruji raised his eyes toward the unseen sky.

"Why? Because the wise know — behind every planetary influence, there is Siva. Time moves. Karma turns. But behind it all… is stillness."

"When life throws storms at you, remember — every graha is but a mask. And behind each mask is the face of the Infinite."

6. Again, at Gangaikonda Cholapuram – The Monolithic Navagraha

"In this same holy site, the grahas are carved on a single monolithic stone, not as individuals — but as a celestial structure.

Not different gods. But one cosmos.

Not separate fates. But one divine intelligence."

Guruji paused, letting the silence reveal what words could not.

Guruji whispered, "Walk the Temple Within"

"Every temple is a manual for living. Some show Surya in the centre — telling you to live by truth. Some place the planets in a line, telling you to walk with discipline.

Some hide them under the sea, telling you to dive deep. Some dissolve them into Siva — telling you to go beyond fate."

"You must not only visit these temples. You must become them. Become the circle. Become the line. Become the sea. Become the stone. Until you, too, stand still — yet move the cosmos."

The Temples That Align the Soul

The devotees sat in stillness, the sound of soft wind rustling through neem trees outside the Buddha Hall.

Guruji said, "Do you think temples are only built of stone?" "No," he whispered. "They are built of longing. Of cosmic insight. Of the need to connect the earth to the stars, the body to the spirit, the self to the vastness."

He paused, letting silence sink in.

"A temple is a mirror of the sky, etched into the land by sages who knew that humans are not meant to live only on Earth. We are also meant to remember where we come from."

And then Guruji gestured toward the south.

"In the sacred land of Tamil Nadu — where river and rhythm, dance and devotion, still breathe together — there lies a chain of nine temples. The Navagraha Sthalams. They are not just places of worship. They are a pilgrimage through your karma, a rebalancing of your inner planets."

1. Suriyanar Kovil – The Temple of the Sun

"The journey begins at Suriyanar Kovil, where the Sun rides his seven horses. There, Surya does not demand devotion — he demands truth."

"Stand before his blazing form and ask yourself: What illusions have I been living under? Where have I hidden my light?

The Sun blesses not with ease, but with clarity. He is the remover of shadows, even those you secretly wish to keep."

2. Thingaloor – The Temple of the Moon

"Next, you go to Thingaloor, where Chandra, the Moon, sits quiet in white marble."

"This temple feels like cool milk in a burning throat. It teaches you how to feel again. Here, you don't pray. You weep. For all the times your emotions betrayed you — or when you betrayed them."

"Chandra teaches: 'The mind is a mirror. Keep it clean, and you will see the stars within you.'"

3. Vaitheeswaran Koil – The Temple of Mars (Angaraka)

"The next stop is fiery Vaitheeswaran, where Mars burns like a warrior who never rests."

"Angaraka is not just the planet of war — he is the planet of courage. This temple heals wounds — not just of the body, but of purpose. It asks: Are you fighting the right battles? Is your anger sacred, or is it poisoning you?"

"Here, Mars becomes medicine — if your rage becomes righteous action."

4. Thiruvenkadu – The Temple of Mercury (Budha)

"At Thiruvenkadu, the breeze changes. This is Mercury's domain — Budha, the god of speech, intelligence, and logic."

"This temple doesn't shout. It whispers truths into your intellect. 'Use your words like mantras,' it says. 'Use your thoughts like bridges, not cages.'"

"For Budha is not just knowledge — he is wisdom with compassion. Clarity without cruelty."

5. Alangudi – The Temple of Jupiter (Guru)

"Ah, but then comes Alangudi. This is not a temple. It is a university of the soul. For here dwells Brihaspati, the Guru of gods."

"This is where you fall at the feet of wisdom, where your pride breaks, and your ego bows."

"Alangudi says: Do not ask for success. Ask for guidance. Do not worship knowledge. Worship the teacher. For without Guru, even the scriptures are silent."

6. Kanjanoor – The Temple of Venus (Shukra)

"At Kanjanoor, you meet Shukra — planet of love, art, wealth, and beauty."

"But he is not the Venus of indulgence — he is the Venus of devotion. The one who gave his eye to restore life to the dead."

"This temple asks: What are you willing to sacrifice for love? Is your love a transaction? Or is it tapas?"

"Here, you learn: True prosperity is not in gold — it is in grace."

7. Thirunallar – The Temple of Saturn (Shani)

Guruji's voice deepened.

"Then comes Thirunallar, and here many pilgrims arrive in fear. For this is the house of Shani, Saturn, the Lord of Time and Karma."

"But let me tell you — Shani is not your enemy. He is your examiner. He takes away only what was never truly yours. He delays not to punish, but to polish."

"Bathe in the temple tank here. Walk barefoot. Let go of pride. And know — when you pass Shani's tests, you emerge invincible."

8. Thirunageswaram – The Temple of Rahu

"At Thirunageswaram, Rahu waits. Mysterious. Shadowy. Obsessive. Powerful."

"Rahu rules illusions, fame, foreign lands, and desires that have no end. He is the serpent's head — hungry, restless."

"But here's the secret — when you stop running after illusions, Rahu becomes your ally. He gives you insight, strategy, and the courage to break social norms and seek moksha."

"This temple teaches you how to see through the mirage."

9. Keezhperumpallam – The Temple of Ketu

"And finally, you reach Keezhperumpallam, where Ketu, the serpent's tail, rests. The headless planet. The moksha graha. The recluse."

"Ketu is detachment, the silent monk, the absence of ego. This temple asks only one question: Are you ready to disappear?"

"Because Ketu blesses not with things — but with freedom from things."

Guruji said, "Walk the Map of Your Soul"

Guruji said, "These temples are more than stones. They are chakras of the Earth, guiding your own journey inward."

"To visit all nine is to walk through your inner sky — from ego to enlightenment. From karma to clarity. From shadow… to the sun."

And then Guruji smiled and whispered, "Do not just visit temples. Become one. Let the nine grahas not revolve outside you… but within. And then — wherever you stand, the cosmos will bow to meet you."

Guruji sat still in silence — his eyes half-closed, as if communing with something beyond sound and beyond form. The devotees watched him, not with impatience but with awe, knowing this quiet was not emptiness — but a fullness too vast for words.

And then, without a word, Guruji slowly rose from his asana. He bowed gently toward the altar, and with a grace born of lifetimes, walked out of the Buddha Hall — as if walking into the stars themselves.

The silence inside was soft, like velvet. Outside, the world had transformed.

The night had descended, draped in dark blue silk. The sky was glittering with stars, blinking like ancient secrets. Clouds drifted like pilgrims across the heavens. A cool breeze stirred, carrying the scent of neem, damp earth, and something older — the scent of longing. Fireflies lit up the night like tiny souls dancing in joy. The croaking of frogs and chirping of crickets played like a soft chant to the moon.

Padma turned to Nita and said, almost in a whisper,

“Let us meet near the fire after dinner.”

And so, the evening unfolded like a sacred ritual.

After dinner — a simple sattvic meal shared in gratitude — the group slowly gathered near the fireplace by the edge of the ashram. The fire crackled gently, casting dancing shadows on their faces. Kiran, Sam, Alice, Sofia, Bhavya, Aarna, Dev, John… they were no longer attendees of a retreat — they were seekers bound by silence and flame.

They were busy discussing fragments of Guruji’s words — karma as echo, time as breath, planets as teachers wearing masks of fate.

Then Sam, who always had a gentle mischief in his tone, turned to Apeksha, the quiet flame among them.

“Tell us a story, Apeksha.”

Apeksha, who had been watching the fire, didn’t answer right away.

She closed her eyes for a long moment, took in the breath of the night, and then she began — slowly, quietly — as if summoning not a tale, but a soul.

The Pot That Held the Sky

“In a small village at the edge of a forgotten forest lived an old potter named Bhairav. He made clay pots not for money, but for silence. Each pot he shaped was like a meditation, a prayer formed with mud and breath.

One day, he heard of a great sage who had come to a nearby mountain. This sage was said to give mystic blessings, glimpses of past lives, and teachings about the soul's journey through the stars.

Bhairav went to see him, carrying his best pot as an offering.

When his turn came, the sage looked at him and asked, 'What do you seek, Potter?'

Bhairav bowed and said, 'I want to hold the sky in one of my pots.'

The others laughed. But the sage did not.

He simply said: 'Then make a pot with no bottom, no top, no sides. Make it with your heart, not your hands. Make it with surrender.'"

Apeksha looked into the fire — its flame danced in her eyes.

"Years passed. Bhairav stopped making pots for people. He began making strange, imperfect ones. Pots with holes. Pots with broken edges. Pots that collapsed mid-process. But each one — he named after a planet.

'This is Shani,' he would say, holding a cracked one. 'This is Rahu,' showing one that was black and had no lid. 'This one is Surya — you can feel its warmth even when it's empty.'

The villagers thought he had gone mad. But children loved him. They would sit around him and hear stories of planets who were not gods but guardians — not judges but guides."

Apeksha's voice became soft now, like a night breeze.

"One day, Bhairav died. The villagers found hundreds of pots in his hut, each named after a planet, a star, a shadow.

And in the centre of the hut — there was one pot, perfectly still, made of some unknown clay. It had no bottom. No top. No sides. Just a ring of emptiness.

When the light of the moon touched it, it shimmered — as if the sky itself was resting inside.

And someone whispered, 'He did it. He held the sky.'"

Tears and Threads of Silence

When Apeksha stopped, no one spoke.

Bhavya wiped her eyes. John looked up at the stars as if searching for Bhairav's hut. Alice pressed her palm to her heart. Even the fire went quiet for a moment, as if bowing.

Then Nita said gently,

"Let us meet again… in the next retreat. The next passage through the planets."

Everyone nodded — not in routine, but with a kind of sacred agreement. Something inside them had shifted.

They weren't just talking about Navagrahas anymore. They were beginning to live them.

The fire crackled again. A shooting star passed. The night was long, yes.

But so was the soul's journey.

And tonight… it had found a home.

Life Coach and Philanthropist

Shree Shambav is the visionary founder of the Shree Shambav Ayur Rakshita Foundation (www.shambav-ayurrakshita.org). He founded this institution with a lofty goal: to recognise human identity across gender, ethnicity, and nationality. Through this organisation, he wants to assist all communities in realising their full potential and the intrinsic beauty of life.

Shree Shambav, a Life Coach, is dedicated to supporting people on their journeys of self-discovery and empowerment. He assists people in discovering who they are, determining what inspires and drives them, and overcoming limiting ideas. His approach clarifies what one wants in life, assisting people through goal-setting and a step-by-step process for achieving them. He empowers people to make deliberate and responsible decisions, allowing them to identify their blind spots and evolve as individuals via the use of numerous strategies and tools.

The foundation's bold, uncompromising, and compassionate ventures are always aimed at initiating the "Inner Transformation" process. They focus on spiritual growth, personal growth, and self-healing while emphasising that true progress lies in "Inclusive Growth and Co-existence." This philosophy drives all their initiatives, encouraging a holistic approach to development and well-being.

Under Shree Shambav's leadership, the foundation has launched several impactful movements:

Shree Shambav Green Movement: This mission is to create a healthy, green, and clean earth through responsible water conservation and greening initiatives. The movement strives to make the world a green paradise by encouraging sustainable living and environmental responsibility.

Shree Shambav Vidya Vedhika (Vizhuthugal): This project aims to help students and children by offering training, books, stationery, and uniforms. It aims to provide the next generation with the tools and resources they need to excel both academically and personally.

Shree Shambav and his foundation exemplify the spirit of compassion, transformation, and inclusive growth via their work, which has a profound impact on individuals and communities around the world. His work exemplifies the power of acknowledging and nourishing the human spirit, creating a world in which everyone can reach their full potential and appreciate the beauty of life.

TESTIMONIALS

Journey of Soul - Karma - "We die in our twenties and are buried at eighty." Remember that nothing can stop someone who refuses to be stopped. "Most people do not fail; they simply give up." Shree Shambav deserves full credit. It allowed me to sit and consider what I might miss out on in life. The author has delved into every aspect of our daily lives. How can a seemingly insignificant change in these seemingly insignificant details bring us such joy? The Soul of Journey teaches you the "art of living" as well as the "art of dying."

Twenty + One Series - The rich cultural heritage offered a host in twenty + one short stories with incredible imagination, morals and values prevalent at a given time, influencing how people respond to a crisis or any situation. The author has recreated images with universal values and morals. The plentiful of fascinating from faraway lands would leave the modern play and story writers a cringe. The book supports trust and immeasurable values instilling hope for the new generations.

Death - "Shree Shambav's 'Death - Light of Life and the Shadow of Death' is an extraordinary masterpiece that delves deep into the profound questions surrounding our existence and mortality. The book's opening statement, 'Nothing ever truly dies; it simply ceases to exist in one form before resuming it in another,' sets the stage for a thought-provoking exploration of death's multifaceted nature. Shambav's remarkable ability to navigate the philosophical complexities of death and our universal fear of it is both enlightening and comforting. This book is a testament to the power of understanding and acceptance."

Whispers of Eternity - "Reading 'Whispers of Eternity' by Shree Shambav was a transformative experience that left me captivated from beginning to end. Each section of this exquisite collection delves into the myriad facets of existence, offering poignant reflections on life, death, and everything in between. Shree Shambav's verses are a testament to the beauty of language and the power of expression, inviting readers to embark on a journey of self-discovery and spiritual awakening. Whether celebrating life's simple joys or grappling with the complexities of human emotion, this book is a timeless companion that speaks to the heart and soul of every reader."

Life Changing Journey Series - "Life Changing Journey Series II Inspirational Quotes" is a remarkable collection that illuminates the path to self-discovery and personal growth. With its inspiring quotes and insightful reflections, this book serves as a beacon of light in a world often shrouded in darkness. Each quote offers wisdom, guidance, and encouragement, reminding readers of their inner strength and resilience. A must-read for anyone seeking inspiration and enlightenment.

Learn To Love Yourself – "A Heartfelt Guide to Authentic Self-Love." "Learn to Love Yourself" invites readers on a transformative journey to embrace their true essence in a world often focused on external validation. Through ten insightful chapters, it gently reveals principles of genuine self-love, guiding readers to deepen their connection with themselves. Beyond surface positivity, it encourages the cultivation of resilient self-acceptance, from embracing one's unique qualities to setting empowering boundaries. With inspiring stories and practical wisdom, this book is a trusted companion on the path to inner peace, fulfilment, and joy, helping readers build lives that reflect their authentic selves.

The Power of Letting Go – This book has been a gift to my spiritual journey. Shree Shambav's insights into attachment, personal growth cycles, and forgiveness are enlightening. The concept of seven-year cycles resonated with me, helping me understand the natural phases of life. I feel more empowered to let go of what no longer serves me and step into a life of freedom and fulfilment. A truly beautiful read!

A Journey of Lasting Peace – "A Journey of Lasting Peace" feels like a trusted friend guiding you through the maze of self-discovery. The 18 transformative principles are both practical and deeply resonant, addressing everything from gratitude practices to the art of letting go. Each chapter is infused with warmth and wisdom, making it easy to apply the concepts to my life. I particularly appreciated the emphasis on physical health's connection to mental well-being; it served as a wake-up call for me to prioritise my health. This book is an invaluable resource for anyone serious about personal growth!

Astrology Unveiled Series – "Profound, Logical, and Inspiring". What stands out in Astrology Unveiled is the author's dedication to making Vedic astrology logical and approachable. Each concept flows naturally into the next, backed by examples and exercises. The insights into karma and life cycles add a philosophical depth rarely seen in astrology books. Perfect for anyone seeking spiritual growth alongside astrological knowledge!

The Entitlement Trap - "Thought-Provoking and Challenging" The book challenges readers to confront their own sense of entitlement, and that's not easy—but it's essential. The Entitlement Trap doesn't offer a one-size-fits-all approach. Instead, it's a thoughtful, layered examination of how entitlement can limit our growth. The chapter on "Defining Your Own Hill" was particularly impactful, as it pushed me to reconsider which challenges are truly worth pursuing. A thought-provoking read for those willing to do the inner work to create a life they can be proud of.

Whispers of a Dying Soul – "A Soul-Stirring Reflection on Life's Unspoken Truths" **-** *Whispers of a Dying Soul: Unspoken Regrets and Unlived Dreams"* is a deeply moving exploration of the unexpressed emotions and unfulfilled aspirations that shape our lives in ways we often don't realise. This book invites readers to confront the powerful, often hidden impact of regret while guiding them through a journey of introspection and healing. Each page opens a space to reflect on the choices that define us—from moments of unspoken love to neglected passions—offering a gentle reminder to live authentically and courageously.

Whispers of the Soul: A Journey Through Haiku - is a mesmerising collection that speaks directly to the heart. Each haiku is a delicate brushstroke capturing life's fleeting beauty and timeless wisdom, inviting readers into moments of deep reflection and peace. This book is a balm for the soul, guiding us to find meaning in stillness and connection in simplicity. The themes of nature, love, and mindfulness echo universal truths, resonating with quiet, powerful grace. It's a book to be savoured slowly, cherished deeply, and returned to often. Truly, a gift for anyone seeking calm and clarity in life's chaos.

Whispers of Silence - Unlocking Inner Power through Stillness by Shree Shambav is a rare gem that beckons readers to pause, reflect, and reconnect with their inner selves. In a world that never stops talking, this book offers a profound exploration of silence—not as a void but as a rich and transformative space.

From the first page, Shree Shambav's writing resonates deeply, blending scientific insights with spiritual wisdom in a way that feels both universal and deeply personal. The author's ability to bridge the tangible and the transcendent makes this book an invaluable guide for anyone navigating the chaos of modern life.

The Power of Words: Transforming Speech, Transforming Lives - "The Power of Words is a profound and enlightening guide that has transformed the way I approach communication. Shree Shambav masterfully uncovers the hidden influence of our words on relationships, self-perception, and overall well-being. This book doesn't just teach you how to speak; it inspires mindful communication that fosters connection and trust. The insights on replacing negative patterns like gossip and judgment with kindness and authenticity are truly life-changing. The practical strategies and engaging narratives make it an invaluable resource for personal and professional growth. A must-read for anyone striving to communicate with intention, clarity, and compassion. Highly recommended!"

The Art of Intentional Living: Minimalism for a Life of Purpose - "The Art of Intentional Living is a refreshing guide to finding clarity in a cluttered world. With practical wisdom and profound insights, it inspires you to simplify, prioritise, and live with purpose. A must-read for anyone seeking balance and fulfilment."

Awakening the Infinite: The Power of Consciousness in Transforming Life - "Awakening the Infinite is a transformative guide that expands the mind and nourishes the soul. With profound insights and practical wisdom, this book beautifully explores the power of consciousness, helping readers connect with their true purpose and inner potential. It is a journey of self-discovery, healing, and spiritual awakening, offering clarity and inspiration at every turn. A must-read for anyone looking to live with greater awareness, meaning, and authenticity."

Beyond the Veil: A Journey Through Life After Death:

"This book touched me in ways few others have—it's not just about death, but about life, meaning, and the vast unknown that connects them. Beyond the Veil offers a graceful blend of science and spirit, inviting us to explore the mystery with awe rather than fear. The stories, insights, and reflections linger in your heart long after the final page. A truly transformative read that brings light on the shadows of mortality. It reminded me that in embracing death, we truly learn how to live."

Bonds Beyond Blood:

"A profoundly moving story that reminds us family is not defined by blood, but by love, sacrifice, and the courage to heal. Every chapter touched my soul with its emotional truth and timeless wisdom. Through joy, grief, and redemption, this book captures the raw beauty of human connection. I saw reflections of my own family in its pages—both the pain and the hope. A powerful, unforgettable read that lingers long after the final word."

A Journey into Spiritual Maturity: 12 Golden Rules for Inner Transformation

"This book is a gentle yet powerful guide that awakened a deeper sense of purpose within me. Each golden rule felt like a mirror reflecting truths I needed to embrace. Shree Shambav's wisdom is timeless, poetic, and profoundly grounding. It's not just a read—it's a journey into the heart of who you truly are. A must-read for anyone seeking lasting peace, clarity, and inner transformation."

The Inner Battlefield: Overcoming the Enemies of the Mind and Soul:

"This book is a powerful revelation—an honest mirror to the battles we fight within. Every chapter is a step closer to clarity, peace, and emotional mastery. Shree Shambav brilliantly transforms ancient wisdom into practical guidance for modern souls. It awakened in me a new strength to face my fears and rise above inner turmoil. A must-read for anyone seeking true inner victory and lasting transformation."

The Seeker's Gold – Unlocking Life's Greatest Treasure

The Seeker's Gold is a soul-stirring masterpiece that goes far beyond the pursuit of wealth—it is a journey into the heart of what truly matters. Each chapter unfolds with poetic wisdom and emotional depth, revealing that life's real treasure is not found in riches but in the transformation of the self. As the protagonist evolves through trials, love, and profound realisations, so does the reader. This book is a mirror for every dreamer, a lantern for every seeker, and a companion for anyone walking the path of purpose. A timeless tale that stays with you long after the final page.

Born to Rise Series I & II :

Born to Rise – Series I & II is a profound awakening—a journey that begins in silence and leads you to the core of your true power.

Series I reshapes your understanding of success, showing that clarity is more valuable than applause, and authenticity more powerful than performance.

Series II takes you deeper, unlocking the mindset and inner strategy behind meaningful, lasting growth—not just in wealth, but in wisdom.

Together, these books are not just guides—they are soul mirrors, revealing the truths you've forgotten and the strength you've always held.

This is more than reading—it's remembering who you are, and rising with purpose, not pressure.

ACKNOWLEDGEMENTS

To my grandfathers, grandmothers, mothers, fathers, aunts, uncles, neighbours, sisters, brothers, friends, and teachers, they poured in endless moral stories, retellings of Ramayana, Mahabharata, Puranas, Upanishads, and so on.

My teachers, neighbours, and kindred souls. Who provided us with a stage to perform wonderful Puranic stories and were gracious enough to acknowledge our efforts.

The artists and translators of epics have served as a source of inspiration, invigorating our spirits, making these works accessible, and enabling us to grasp the profound depths and deeper dimensions they contain.

I also cherish the stimulating conversations; I had with my wonderful mothers, Punitha Muniswamy and Uma Devi.

Our family's youngest member, Aadhya, who always overwhelmed me with questions, inspired this book.

I would likewise prefer to express gratitude to Mr Sivakumar, Mrs Roopa Sivakumar, Mr Akshaya Rajesh,

Ms Akshatha Rajesh, Ms Apeksha Prabhu, Mr Akanksh Prabhu, Mr Nikash Sarasambi, and Mrs Spoorthi Nikash for their valuable inputs.

I must thank Mr Rajesh, Mr Savan Prabhu, Mrs Revathi Rajesh, Mrs Rajani Sarasambi, and Mrs Manju Reshma, who encouraged me and often suggested writing a book. Their unwavering belief that I had something valuable to offer kept me going during my writing sessions.

Love you all,

Shree Shambav

Web: www.shambav.org

Email: shreeshambav@gmail.com

9 789334 336719

Printed at Repro India Ltd.